Subverting Syria

How CIA Contra Gangs and NGOs Manufacture, Mislabel and Market Mass Murder

Tony Cartalucci

Nile Bowie

2012

Subverting Syria
How CIA Contra Gangs and NGO's
Manufacture, Mislabel and Market Mass Murder

Copyright Tony Cartalucci & Nile Bowie 2012
Published by Progressive Press
September 2012

ISBN: 1-61577-5579 EAN: 9781-61577-5576

BISAC Subject Area Codes

HIS026000   HISTORY / Middle East
HIS027180   HISTORY / Military / Special Forces
POL045000   POLITICAL SCIENCE / Colonialism & Post-Colonialism

The cover image displays the tactical progression of "soft warfare." First, introduce gangs of terrorists, calling them "freedom fighters." Second, the bandits spread chaos with attacks, such as this car bombing. Third, after cynically pinning their own atrocities on the Syrian government and spreading this Big Lie worldwide through the corporate-controlled media, they call for intervention by NATO (Russia, with its only warm-water naval base in Syria, vetoed all UN resolutions for an attack.) Finally, a proud, prosperous and independent nation is pummeled into submission by American weapons of mass destruction.

The images form a letter L, spelling LIBYA.

The Syrian "uprising" is a cynical US-engineered plot using provocateurs, mercenaries, Wahhabi fanatics, corrupt NGO's and the global media. The US, NATO and the feudal emirates are out to smash this independent Arab state that spends on human welfare and refuses to surrender to Israel.

The US and Saudi-financed plot turns on the tactic of "Countergangs." Terrorists – mercenaries and irregulars, the "CIA foreign legion" – shoot both demonstrators and police, blow up buildings, massacre innocent villagers – and then blame the carnage on the targeted government.

NGO's like NED, the "National Endowment for Democracy" (funded by US State Dept, Geo. Soros, Ford Foundation etc) promote "activists," whose leaders are ambitious sociopaths, eagerly carving out a piece of the carcass for the moment the state is brought down. The corporate lapdog media, cogs in the military-industrial complex, lap up and magnify the Big Lie, creating a fake "reality" that the average person has little chance of seeing through.

Subverting Syria is a warning of the horror that the "Empire of the Almighty Dollar" is preparing to bring down upon Syria, the same horror of last year's obscene war on Libya, in which an egalitarian state was trampled into mud, blood and chaos under the banner of human rights and a pack of vicious lies.

Subverting Syria reveals how the crusade to destroy Syria follows tactics explicitly set out in the Pentagon's Unconventional Warfare Manual.

- fund NGO's to create a climate of protest in the target country

- provocateurs organize demonstrations, then fire on protesters and security forces alike to stoke violence

- staged and mislabeled video footage creates the illusion of repression

- mass media endlessly repeat the Big Lie that the nation's leader is a brutal dictator killing his own people. "Give a dog a bad name and hang him."

- invade border towns with special forces death squads, the CIA Foreign Legion of Al Qaeda psychopaths, fanatics and guns for hire

- fabricate pretexts for military intervention by the UN, or NATO

- bomb the country into the stone age, to be conquered by NATO's Islamic terrorist puppets

- eradicate Arab socialism and government for the people, replacing it with a corrupt clique beholden to Wall Street and London bankers

- isolate Lebanon, Palestine, Iraq and Iran, giving free rein for Greater Israel to dominate the Middle East

- US corporations write multi-billion-dollar contracts for "reconstruction" and "security"

Subverting Syria shows how wars are engineered by manipulation of the kinder instincts of mankind, hoodwinking and harnessing pacifist and leftist forces – entrapping them in the service of mass murder and the global dictatorship of the money power.

Table of Contents

Publisher's Note   5

Author's Note   7

Chapter 1: The Architecture of Insurgency   8

Chapter 2: Perception Management and Psychological Warfare   48

Chapter 3: The Prospect of Regional War   71

Conclusion   105

Publisher's Note

This book is an urgent attempt to alert the world, especially people of good will, to the impending horror that the "Empire of the Almighty Dollar" is preparing to bring down upon Syria, and many another nation that strives for independence. Syria in the cross-hairs to suffer the same horror of last year's war on Libya, that unspeakable obscenity of history and bottomless pit of hypocrisy, in which the most egalitarian state in the region was trampled into mud, blood and chaos under the banner of human rights and a pack of vicious lies.

The rank obscenity of these wars lies in great part in the manipulation of the kinder instincts of mankind, the hoodwinking and harnessing of those who otherwise tend to oppose "interventions", especially pacifist and leftist forces—entrapping them in the service of mass murder and the global dictatorship of the money power. One can only imagine the smug sneers on the faces of the think-tankers, as they watch their nominal opponents lining up *en masse* to demand the dirty work be done.

The modus operandi is the *Countergang*, as a growing number of distinguished authors have documented. Terrorists—mercenaries and irregulars, the "CIA foreign legion"—blow up buildings, massacre innocents, and then **blame the carnage on the targeted government**. NGOs like the "National Endowment for Democracy" (NED) promote so-called activists, whose leaders are ambitious sociopaths, eagerly carving out a piece of the carcass for the moment the state is brought down. The mainstream and even the alternative media eagerly lap up and amplify the Big Lie, creating a substitute "reality" that the average person has little chance of seeing through.

A difficult message to get across in time as the juggernaut of genocide bears down on plucky, unlucky Syria. But we have to try.

President Assad the Younger of Syria has taken on the most delicate task: attempting to dismantle dictatorship, introduce reforms and loosen controls, without losing control—and without surrendering the nation's independence to global neo-colonialism. Difficult enough to carry out, even without the rampant foreign subversion that it invites. Indeed, the allegedly all-powerful Western nations, including the United States, have not mastered this trick. Despite, or due to, the façade of freedom and democracy we enjoy in the West, we are all "in debt" to the same clique of power brokers and global financiers who lend us our own money at interest, and who pull our strings to unleash our weapons of mass destruction on any country that won't dance to their music.

The reasoning for this appalling situation is simple enough; you could call it "Leonard's first and last law of political science." There is only one way the 1% can beat the 99% in the game of life, and that is by cheating. Because clearly, under any scheme of fair play, we the 99% must surely impose our will and our self-interest. We can only be defeated by deception, manipulation, entrapment, conditioning, pandering to the worst in people, all the tricks in the book. And all those tricks sum up to the equation that *the world presented to us—through the means controlled by the 1%—is a distortion, often even a fabrication*. Their only answer is to sneer that this is a conspiracy theory. Of course it is a conspiracy—how else could they go about it.

So all the world's a stage—that we have to see through to see the truth. Nothing is as it seems in the mainstream. This book will prove that axiom in one single, but tragically significant, facet: the Big Lie about Syria.

And thanks to you, dear reader—for engaging the side of truth in the battle.

John-Paul Leonard,

June 2012

Author's Note

Thank you for reading *"Subverting Syria: How CIA Contra Gangs and NGO's Manufacture, Mislabel and Market Mass Murder."* Your interest and attention is highly appreciated by the authors of this book. The purpose of this document is to provide an accurate historical record of the conflict in Syria. This was a challenging task, namely because I was approached to create this project while the conflict was still ongoing. The individuals involved in this project found it necessary to compile our various articles and conclusions into one definitive product and, because the fighting in Syria has not ceased, it is necessary to produce expanded editions in the future.

This book is based on the articles and research of Tony Cartalucci, an independent journalist and editor of *Land Destroyer Report* based in Bangkok, Thailand. My role in this book was to expand these articles and compile them into a coherent narrative, a difficult task for any writer. Inevitably, much of my research appears within these pages to give readers the most in-depth, formulated, and critical account of events in Syria we can offer. After compiling the chapters, Eric Draitser, a New York City-based journalist and editor of *StopImperialism.com,* contributed by editing and proofreading the text. I worked for two months out of my apartment in Kuala Lumpur, Malaysia to produce this document.

The authors of this book hope that this project encourages others to forge ties with like-minded people from around the world, and constructively collaborate to bring attention to compelling issues and injustices. This book isn't exactly bedside reading, but it inevitably contains very important analysis and information that needs to be more broadly exposed. It is written in such a way that may initially confuse readers who are unfamiliar with the names, locations, and events we cite. Our best efforts have been made to make this information as accessible and well defined as possible.

Opponents and critics of this information will dismiss our research and conclusions, and familiarly brand us "conspiracy theorists" or apologists of the Syrian government. The makers of this book do not endorse any political party or organization, nor do we receive funding for this work from anyone. These conclusions are our own, and ultimately, we believe in the primacy of national sovereignty, respect for international law, and the right of the Syrian people to decide their own political future without such a future being imposed on them.

Once again, thank you for reading this book and we hope this information improves your understanding of the situation.

This work is dedicated to those innocents who suffered untimely deaths in Syria and elsewhere.

Nile Bowie

August 24, 2012

Chapter 1: The Architecture of Insurgency

"There is another type of warfare—new in its intensity, ancient in its origin—war by guerrillas, subversives, insurgents, assassins; war by ambush instead of by combat, by infiltration instead of aggression, seeking victory by eroding and exhausting the enemy instead of engaging him. It preys on unrest."

John F. Kennedy

35th President of the United States

Several months of political turmoil in Tunisia triggered the series of events referred to as the "Arab Spring," which then engulfed several countries in North Africa. Among those who took to the streets intending to peacefully demonstrate, were local dissidents that received training, funding and material assistance from foreign powers through organizations funded largely by the US State Department. As these movements garnered the attention of the international media, unverified reports of excessive government violence were used to tarnish the image of national governments in the region. Media enterprises such as *Al-Jazeera* and *FOX News* did their part to condition public opinion in an effort to build support for Western-sanctioned opposition groups. Dissident forces would later openly receive arms and material assistance from abroad, in order to wage insurrectionary guerilla warfare against the governing authorities of those countries.

One of the organizations involved in recruiting, training, and supporting youth activists ahead of the "Arab Spring" was described in an April 2011 *New York Times* article.[1] The organization, Movements.org, or Alliance of Youth Movements, would later be described admitting to US funding and involvement in the "Arab Spring" uprisings. The article implicates Freedom House, the National Endowment for Democracy, and two of its satellite organizations, the International Republican Institute, and the National Democratic Institute, in recruiting, training, and supporting the unrest starting as early as 2008. While the *New York Times* article doesn't mention the organization by name, it links to an official US State Department announcement titled, "Announcement on Alliance of Youth Movements Summit," that most certainly does.[2] The Alliance of Youth Movements is a corporate-sponsored "coup college" of sorts, training activists to subvert and topple governments on the US State Department's behalf.

On February 26th, 2011, the US-based Brookings Institution issued a report titled, "Libya's Test of the New International Order," which argued in favor of intervention in Libya, describing the undertaking as "a test that the international community has to pass." Failure to do so would, in the words of Brookings Doha Center Director Salman Shaikh, "shake further the faith of the people's region in the emerging international order and the primacy of international law." Succeeding would, as the report states, "demonstrably draw a line in the sand to deter other

---

[1] U.S. Groups Helped Nurture Arab Uprisings, The New York Times, April 14, 2011
[2] Announcement on Alliance of Youth Movements Summit, America.Gov Archive, November 20, 2008

Arab autocrats who resort to attacking their people rather than dialogue and genuine reforms." By reforms, Brookings is referring to Libya's integration into the "international system," where protectionist economic policies would be pushed aside to allow foreign governments and multinational corporations to usurp the countries' sovereignty and vast natural resources.[3]

The government of Muammar Gaddafi had been accused of using targeted airstrikes against gatherings of unarmed demonstrators, as cited by a concentrated stream of unverified activist testimony, alleging the perpetration of state-sponsored crimes against humanity. In late March 2011, following the passage of UN Resolution 1973 which mandated the enforcement of a no-fly-zone over Libya, NATO launched a bombing campaign in support of Libya's armed rebels, under the auspices of "protecting civilians." Former French President Nicholas Sarkozy would echo Brookings' sentiments, stating:

Every ruler should understand, and especially every Arab ruler should understand that the reaction of the international community and of Europe will from this moment on each time be the same: we will be on the side of peaceful protesters who must not be repressed with violence.[4]

The United Nations passed Resolution 1973 amid the first reports of insurrectionary violence in the southern Syrian city of Daraa. While the mainstream media portrayed armed rebels instigating violence against Syrian security forces as "peaceful protestors," US Senator Joe Lieberman would threaten Syria with foreign military intervention. In Daraa, protesters torched the Ba'ath Party headquarters and destroyed cars parked along the street, while two protesters were reportedly killed as they attempted to set ablaze another government building in the city of Latakia. It is difficult to understand how any responsible government should be expected to allow foreign-funded mobs to commit widespread arson and vandalism with the expressed goal of removing the standing government from power. Undoubtedly, the violence exhibited by the protesters was designed to intentionally provoke Syrian security forces attempting to maintain order.

However excessively or appropriately the Syrian security forces reacted to the violence, the mainstream media and Western politicians attempted to leverage legitimacy away from Damascus, citing the violence as the justification for President Bashar al-Assad to step aside. Disturbingly, the continued perpetuation of violence and disorder has been attributed to hired provocateurs, which are often employed to kill protesters and security forces alike, creating an internationally sensationalized bloodbath, designed to escalate both the protests and international pressure on the state. An article published by The *Sydney Morning Herald* entitled, "Bloodbath New Threat to Assad" stated that the instability in southern Syria has left the regime "staggering." Additionally, it invited "stern" criticism from US President Barack Obama stating:

---

[3] Libya's Test of the New International Order, Brookings Institution, February 26, 2011
[4] Sarkozy warns Arab rulers about Libya precedent, EuObserver, March 25, 2011

Instead of listening to their own people, President Assad is blaming outsiders while seeking Iranian assistance in repressing Syria's citizens through the same brutal tactics that have been used by his Iranian allies.[5]

While the Syrian government initially credited "armed groups" and rooftop snipers with committing acts of violence against protestors and security forces, reports by outlets such as *Al-Jazeera* relied solely on anonymous accounts of the opposition, who have continued to push the official narrative of an unprovoked government crackdown on Syria's civilian population. *Al-Jazeera*'s article, "'Nine killed' at Syria funeral processions," included testimony from one of their correspondents on the ground who stated:

[People marching on an overpass] were met with a hail of gunfire, many people certainly wounded directly in front of us, cars turned around, and I can tell you it was an incredibly chaotic scene, and it seems as though pretty much everyone down here in the southern part of the country is now carrying weapons. It is unclear who was firing at whom, that's part of the confusion ... but clearly a very violent incident now being carried out here in the south of the country.[6]

Though cryptic, this description seemed to corroborate the Syrian government's assertion that they weren't the only ones with guns. As reports of mystery gunmen and rooftop snipers continued to emerge, events that unfolded halfway around the world in Thailand shared identical patterns with the state-sponsored destabilization being undertaken in southern Syria.

On April 10th, 2010, the Thai military attempted to disperse red-shirted supporters of billionaire telecommunications tycoon and exiled political leader Thaksin Shinawatra at Bangkok's "Democracy Monument". The military employed the use of water cannons and rubber bullets when a group of unknown gunmen intervened with a combination of grenade attacks and sniper fire that killed the Thai military's Colonel Romklao and six other soldiers. Troops immediately fell back in disarray, while protesters were divided in confusion and adulation. The mystery gunmen weaved through the protesters firing sporadically at Thai troops who returned fire. In total, 23 died. While the protesters were entirely unaware of the gambit, it is unlikely that even the security guards knew of the impending attack, as many immediately rushed in to protect fallen soldiers from aggressive protesters, while gun battles continued elsewhere.

It was quite clear that a highly trained, well prepared third party was involved, and unlike in Syria where few foreigners venture and fewer cameras seem to be sending back footage, both foreign and domestic, amateur and professional footage caught the melee on tape. Initial blanket denials by protest leaders quickly became piecemeal confessions as footage of these "men in black" filtered out. International spokesman for the protesters, Sean Boonpracong, told *Reuters* that elements of the army were with their movement, including the black-clad mystery gunmen that took part in the April 10th bloodbath.[7] He stated, "They are a secret unit within the army

---

[5] Bloodbath New Threat to Assad, The Sydney Morning Herald, April 23, 2011
[6] 'Nine killed' at Syria funeral processions, Al-Jazeera, April 23, 2011
[7] Red means stop, and anger, in vibrant Thai protest, Reuters, April 2010

that disagrees with what's going on. Without them, the black-clad men, there would have been a whole lot more deaths and injuries." The suspected leader of these gunmen, renegade general Khattiya Sawasdipol, known as "Seh Daeng," further damned earlier denials by admitting to commanding 300 armed men trained for "close encounters," armed with M79 grenade launchers, before withdrawing his comment in later interviews.[8]

From April 10th, until the widespread arson that marked the end of the protests on May 19th, daily and nightly gun battles, grenade attacks, and sniper fire would claim the lives of 91 people. This included 9 soldiers and police, a woman killed by an M79 grenade attack, and at least one protester who died of smoke inhalation while looting a building lit by fellow protesters. The remaining 80 deaths included journalists, bystanders, medical workers, and protesters caught in the crossfire. To explain why such a bloodbath was necessary, Sean Boonpracong, after admitting the mystery gunmen were working on his movement's behalf, gave another breathtaking confession in an April 24th interview. When asked why protest leaders had turned down a government offer to hold fresh elections in 9 months, he responded by saying that, after the April 10th incident, they felt Thai Prime Minister Abhisit Vejjajiva's hands were "tainted with blood" and that it would be best if the Thai Parliament was dissolved. He continued by stating the protest's demands had changed to immediate dissolution as well as Prime Minister Abhisit's leaving the country.

Tragic events in Thailand provide a vivid example – complete with brazen admissions – of how "mystery gunmen" for hire were used to foment grotesque spectacles used to distort realities in favor of opposition groups supported from abroad. Their violence serves two purposes, to create enough chaos and bloodshed to force a government to step down, or to justify escalating anger and violence amongst the unsuspecting regular rank and file protesters. In the Syrian context, reports of mystery gunmen and "death squads" escalated the situation dramatically, at the expense of thousands of civilian causalities. Reports issued by Iran's *Al-Alam* Arabic Language News Network described how snipers linked to Saudi Arabia and the American CIA were operating in Syria to purposefully assassinate protesters in order to expand unrest. The reports describe a motorcycle driver delivering a sniper to a building before speeding off. Once in position, the sniper fires on protesters. Syrian security forces surround the building and a shootout allegedly takes place. The text concludes stating that the sniper is injured and taken to a hospital.

Al-Alam's report and footage would corroborate both government and eyewitness accounts cited by international media, stating that "snipers on rooftops" were shooting at protesters. While "rights activists" assume the snipers are security forces, the government maintains that gunmen have opened fire on protesters and security forces alike. A *CNN* report from April 2011 cited a Syrian official who stated that, "an unknown 'armed group on rooftops shot at protesters and security forces." [9] Activists said they believe the people on the rooftops were snipers from security forces but have put forth no evidence beyond "witness accounts." China's *XinhuaNet*

[8] 'Red Commander' saw himself as Thai William Wallace, The Age, May 19, 2010
[9] Reports of funeral, police shootings raise tensions in Syria, CNN, April 05, 2011

reported multiple incidents across Syria where armed gangs had clashed with security forces killing members on both sides. One attack claimed the lives of 8 bystanders. Official state media in Syria presented evidence that groups had been caught with non-Syrian SIM cards in their phones along with equipment used to stage acts of violence.[10]

An April 2011 Op-Ed released by the Brookings Institution titled, "In Syria, Assad Must Exit the Stage," describes how the cycle of violence initiated by "mysterious gunmen" targeting funerals is cited as the line Assad had crossed - which now requires his departure from power. The article states:

With the cycle of ever-increasing protests met by regime violence and then more funerals intensifying in all areas of the country, it is time for Assad, the 'Hamlet' of the Arab world, to consider his future. It is time for him and those who influence him abroad to search for a swift and orderly exit.[11]

By late April, NATO continued to enforce a no-fly zone over Libya while conducting air strikes in support of the militant opposition. As was the case with Hosni Mubarak and Muammar Gaddafi before him, US Senators John McCain, Lindsey Graham, and Joe Lieberman issued a joint statement declaring that that Bashar al- Assad had "lost the legitimacy to remain in power in Syria." They continued by stating:

Rather than hedging our bets or making excuses for the Assad regime, it is time for the United States, together with our allies in Europe and around the world, to align ourselves unequivocally with the Syrian people in their peaceful demand for a democratic government.[12]

The US Senators' statements remain unequivocally dishonest, as McCain and Graham are both members of the International Republican Institute, an organization openly implicated by the *New York Times* in funding opposition groups who took part in the "Arab Spring." Likewise, Lieberman is a member of the Neo-Conservative lobbying firm deceptively named the "Foundation for Defense of Democracies (FDD)," which features a host of Project for a New American Century (PNAC) signatories including William Kristol, Richard Perle, James Woolsey, and Paula Dobriansky, as well as Council on Foreign Relations members, Newt Gingrich and Charles Krauthammer. While members of the American political establishment readily denounce foreign governments for their general non-acquiescence, the substantial support given to political opposition groups has worked to foment civil unrest and enflame domestic tensions in target nations around the world.

Washington had seemingly reached a consensus regarding the need for regime change in Syria and, by 2011, it became clear that they were willing to employ their long-standing connections to Islamist networks such as the Muslim Brotherhood, to bolster opposition forces and leverage control away from Damascus. The *Washington Post* reports that, since 2005, both the Bush and Obama administrations contributed funding to Syrian opposition groups affiliated with the Muslim

10 Mobile Phones Using non-Syrian SIM Cards, SANA News Agency, April 23, 2011
11 In Syria, Assad Must Exit the Stage, Brookings Institution, April 27, 2011
12 Obama Under Pressure to Call for Syrian Leader's Ouster, FOX News, April 29, 2011

Brotherhood. The article cites how the campaign to provide support to anti-government groups in Syria transcended two presidential administrations:

The U.S. money for Syrian opposition figures began flowing under President George W. Bush after he effectively froze political ties with Damascus in 2005. The financial backing has continued under President Obama, even as his administration sought to rebuild relations with Assad. Syrian authorities "would undoubtedly view any U.S. funds going to illegal political groups as tantamount to supporting regime change," read an April 2009 cable signed by the top-ranking U.S. diplomat in Damascus at the time. "A reassessment of current U.S.-sponsored programming that supports anti-[government] factions, both inside and outside Syria, may prove productive," the cable said.

Edgar Vasquez, a State Department spokesman, said the Middle East Partnership Initiative has allocated $7.5 million for Syrian programs since 2005. A cable from the embassy in Damascus, however, pegged a much higher total — about $12 million — between 2005 and 2010. The cables report persistent fears among U.S. diplomats that Syrian state security agents had uncovered the money trail from Washington.[13]

In 2002, then US Under Secretary of State John Bolton, would add Syria to the growing "Axis of Evil." It would be later revealed that Bolton's threats against Syria would manifest themselves as covert funding and support for opposition groups inside of Syria. In an April 2011 *AFP* report, Michael Posner, the Assistant US Secretary of State for Democracy, Human Rights and Labor, stated that the "US government has budgeted $50 million in the last two years to develop new technologies to help activists protect themselves from arrest and prosecution by authoritarian governments." The report went on to explain that the US "organized training sessions for 5,000 activists in different parts of the world. A session held in the Middle East about six weeks ago gathered activists from Tunisia, Egypt, Syria and Lebanon who returned to their countries with the aim of training their colleagues there." Posner would add, "They went back and there's a ripple effect." That ripple effect, of course, describes the course of events that led to Syria's internal political crisis escalating into an anarchic sectarian war.[14]

Years of covert support to Syrian opposition groups from the US State Department remains significant, especially considering that recipients were reportedly affiliated with the Syrian Muslim Brotherhood, a group that has historically attempted multiple uprisings since the 1960's and long condemned Syria's minority Alawi-Shia groups as heretics. *Global Post's* article titled, "Free Syrian Army plagued by division," confirms that segments of the militants battling Syrian security forces are being drawn from the Brotherhoods' ranks. The Muslim Brotherhood is an organization almost as omnipresent as MI6 or the CIA and coincidentally is working in tandem with other US-funded "youth activists" across the region.[15]

---

[13] U.S. secretly backed Syrian opposition groups, cables released by WikiLeaks show, The Washington Post, April 18, 2011
[14] US trains activists to evade security forces, AFP, April 8, 2011
[15] Free Syrian Army plagued by division, Global Post, March 10, 2012

The Muslim Brotherhood's history in Syria goes back decades. According to a Brandeis University publication titled, "The Syrian Muslim Brotherhood and the Asad Regime," in 1979 the Brotherhood, also called the "Ikhwan," attacked and massacred 32 Syrian military cadets. This was part of a larger campaign of violence conducted by the Brotherhood that also included assassination attempts against the Syrian president. The escalating campaign of violence was the primary impetus for their cornering and destruction at the hands of the Syrian military in the city of Hamah in 1982. After their defeat, many members fled Syria and established operations in London.[16]

While corporate media outlets and government press releases accused the Syrian government of killing civilians, domestic Syrian press reported the presence of armed terrorist groups, brandishing up-to-date American and Israeli weapons, roaming the Damascene countryside committing blind acts of terror by setting off explosive devices and kidnapping civilians. The original Arab League Observer Mission to Syria report conducted from December 24th, 2011 to January 18th, 2012 confirms the allegations of Syrian state media.[17] The contents of the report were largely overlooked by the mainstream media after Qatar disputed its findings, the only nation to do so in the Arab League's Ministerial Committee. The report unwaveringly concluded that the Syrian government was not conducting a campaign of repression against peaceful protestors. Furthermore, the report credits armed gangs with the bombing of civilian buses, trains carrying diesel oil, police buses, and the bombing of bridges and pipelines. During an interview with Arab League observer Ahmed Manaï, he condemns the Arab League for its failure to acknowledge the observers' findings, stating:

The Arab League is entirely discredited by burying the report of its own observers' mission and its appeal to the Security Council. It missed the opportunity to participate in the settlement of the Syrian affair. All it can offer in the future will be worthless.[18]

Since late April 2011, the Syrian government began frequently issuing reports of mysterious gunmen who were opening fire on protesters and security forces from rooftops. While the Western mainstream media attempted to dismiss these frequently cited reports as groundless Syrian propaganda, the rising death toll of government troops certainly could not be attributed to "unarmed civilians. By early March 2011, multiple reports surfaced accusing NATO of training rebel fighters in Libya and using unmarked aircrafts to transport armed fighters to air bases in Turkey to assist the Free Syrian Army. The *Examiner* reports:

The fighters are being recruited from the various Libyan militias, which fought the Gaddafi regime. About 4,000 have volunteered to fight with anti-Assad forces, accepting the offer of $1,000 signing bonus, in addition to a monthly wage of $450 – paid for, according to some unconfirmed reports in freshly printed 'crisp' brand new American $100 dollar bills, leading some to believe that this is US taxpayer funds being used here. Upon landing in Turkey, the Libyan fighters and the arms shipments

---

16 The Syrian Muslim Brotherhood and the Asad Regime, Brandeis University, December 2010

17 Report of Arab League Observer Mission, League of Arab States, Janurary 27, 2012

18 The observer Ahmed Manaï "The Arab League has buried the observers report on Syria," Nawaat, February 08, 2012

are offloaded from the planes and then loaded on trucks to Free Syrian Army bases, most of which are located in the Iskenderun region of Turkey on the border of northwestern Syria. They receive military training from Western, Turkish and Arab army instructors, as well as civilian security consultants and ex-special forces trainers from the US, Britain, France, Italy, Saudi Arabia, Jordan and Qatar.[19]

In "Libya's new rulers offer weapons to Syrian rebels," The *Telegraph* reported that members of the Libyan National Transition Council met with members of the Syrian National Council to offer money, training and weapons to Syrian rebel fighters.[20] According to Libyan military sources, Abdulhakim Belhadj, head of the Tripoli Military Council and the former leader of the militant Libyan Islamic Fighting Group (US State Department listed Terrorist Organization #28), met with Free Syrian Army leaders in Istanbul, on the orders of Mustafa Abdul Jalil, President of the National Transition Council. Belhadj, who had fought with the Taliban against US troops in Afghanistan, was captured by the CIA in Malaysia in 2003 and extradited to Libya where Muammar Gaddafi had him imprisoned. Studies conducted by the Combating Terrorism Center at the US Military Academy at West Point analyzing foreign militants who came to Iraq to fight American and coalition forces conclude that Libya provided the highest number of foreign fighters per capita.[21] The vast majority of fighters came from Dernah, a town about 200 km east of Benghazi, in which an Islamic emirate was declared when the rebellion against Gaddafi started. Libyan rebel leader Abdulhakim Belhadj would also admit that fighters from his Libyan Islamic Fighting Group were the second-largest brigade of foreign fighters in Iraq. The *Irish Times* would report that Mahdi al-Harati, a deputy chief of the Libyan Military Council, had resigned from his duties in Tripoli to oversee the Free Syrian Army.[22] This vast body of documented evidence and admissions show the direct connection between the Western-backed militant forces that were tasked with toppling the Gaddafi regime, and those working toward the same outcome in Syria.

As Syrian state TV broadcasted reports showing seized weapons stockpiles and confessions by terrorists describing how they obtained arms from foreign sources, Western media entirely dismissed the reports and continued to undermine the legitimacy of the Syrian state media. Within the pages of the *Asharq Al-Awsat* newspaper (based in London and funded by Saudi Arabia), Hillary Clinton joined Barack Obama, Nicholas Sarkozy, and David Cameron in the unusual trend of Western political leaders writing newspaper editorials in an attempt to reinforce the ever-changing, contradictory official narrative of events in Syria. Clinton's article entitled, "There is no going back in Syria," states:

If President Assad believes that the protests are the work of foreign instigators – as his government has claimed – he is wrong. It is true that some Syrian soldiers have

---

[19] US helping to train and arm Islamic mercenaries to fight in Syria, The Examiner, March 9, 2012
[20] Libya's new rulers offer weapons to Syrian rebels, The Telegraph, November 25, 2011
[21] Al-Qa'iada's Foreign Fighters in Iraq, Combating Terrorism Center At West Point, December 19, 2007
[22] Libyan-Irish commander resigns as deputy head of Tripoli military council, The Irish Times, October 11, 2011

been killed, and we regret the loss of those lives too. But the vast majority of casualties have been unarmed civilians.[23]

Clinton's own admission that Syrian soldiers have died indicates that indeed, armed individuals were amongst the protesters. Extraordinarily, Clinton manages to both confirm and deny the violent nature of the protests by stating that while Syrian troops have died, the vast majority of the deaths (according to unverified reports by the protesters themselves) were "unarmed civilians." Throughout Hillary Clinton's lengthy diatribe, she failed to even once condemn the violence she hinted at amongst the opposition. Articles such as the *Christian Science Monitor*'s "Has Syria's peaceful uprising turned into an insurrection?" attempted to spin increasing reports of Syrian rebel groups committing violence in an effort to negate the insurrectionary nature of the Syrian conflict since its origins in Daraa.[24] The article suggested that the Syrian government is unjustifiably using violence against its own people and has thus, "brought it on themselves" in regard to the increasing violence exercised by the militant opposition. Syria's mobilization of entire armored divisions and military aircraft would not be necessary if protesters were merely carrying placards and chanting slogans.

In June 2011, France would admit to violating the terms of UN Resolution 1973 by arming Libya's rebels, who were referred to as "peaceful protestors" until the establishment of the no-fly zone, from which point they were lent additional weapons when it became clear they could not take the country by themselves. By late July 2011, violence continued unimpeded in Syria as supporters of the rebel fighters, perpetuating the ongoing unrest, would defend their actions by claiming that protesters were merely defending themselves against a genocidal government, even as mainstream outlets such as *Sky News* report that a Syrian army assault in Hamah "prompted opposition gunmen to fire machine guns and set police stations on fire." Turkey claimed it seized a Syrian ship allegedly carrying weapons, declaring its intentions to enforce an "arms embargo" on the state for its "brutal crackdown on the country's uprising." Turkey's Prime Minister, Recep Tayyip Erdoğan, stated that Turkey was "coordinating its efforts" with Washington in its bid to pressure Syrian president Bashar al-Assad to resign by enforcing a strict regime of sanctions against the nation.[25]

While the Turkish state condemns the alleged reports of state violence committed by the Syrian government, Ankara itself has been waging a decades-long campaign of violence against its own armed uprising in predominately Kurdish areas bordering Syria, Iraq, and Iran. In fact, at one point, the US allowed Turkish tanks to cross into American-occupied Iraq to attack villages suspected of harboring armed Kurdish separatists in 2008, mirroring the very tactics Erdoğan has condemned Syria for allegedly using. The *Guardian* reported in a 2008 article, "Iraq demands Turkey withdraw from border conflict with Kurds," that the conflict had been raging since 1984 and had cost the lives of 40,000 people.[26] While Turkey's Prime Minister

---

[23] Op-Ed: "There Is No Going Back in Syria," U.S Department of State Official Blog, June 17, 2011
[24] Has Syria's peaceful uprising turned into an insurrection?, Christian Science Monitor, June 9, 2011
[25] Syrian Civilians 'Killed In Tank Attack', Sky News, July 31, 2011
[26] Iraq demands Turkey withdraw from border conflict with Kurds, The Guardian, February 28, 2008

lectured neighboring Syria on its bid to crush foreign-funded, armed militants attempting to overthrow the Assad government, the Turkish government was preparing to augment its compliment of Israeli drones with a deployment of US Predator drones on its soil to combat Kurdish militants operating within its territory.

The *Associated Press* reported in an article titled, "Turkey: US likely to deploy Predator drones," that Turkey was "pressing for the drones in an escalating war against Kurdish rebels." Turkey, in addition to deploying drones and rolling tanks into towns suspected of harboring militants, has also strafed suspected rebel strongholds with airstrikes and conducted sweeping nationwide mass arrests. In other words, Turkey has historically committed the same aggressive acts that Syria was accused of committing in its effort to overcome insurgent violence directed at the state and civilians.[27] *Amnesty International, Human Rights Watch*, and a myriad of disingenuous human rights advocate groups remained predictably silent regarding Turkey's actions, even as Ankara unilaterally crossed borders in pursuit of militants, an egregious transgression against its neighbors' sovereignty. Groups such as Freedom House, *Reporters Without Borders*, and International Federation for Human Rights (FIDH), all of which receive funding from the US State Department and Wall Street financiers such as George Soros, demonstrate the way in which these condemnations are selectively applied.

Syrian Kurds have allegedly participated in the uprising against the Assad government, further expanding the irony of Turkey's intrusions into Syria's domestic affairs. The *Jerusalem Post* also reported that Kurdish "activists" living abroad, convened in Europe to call on Syria's Kurdish minority to join the uprising.[28] The Kurds have been the historical proxy of choice for Western powers and their client states to destabilize and harass target nations throughout the Middle East with a certain degree of "plausible deniability." By early September 2011, *Al-Jazeera* (a network funded by the government of Qatar, a nation implicated in providing arms to the Syrian opposition) laid to rest the fable that Syria's protesters are "peaceful, pro-democracy demonstrators," by admitting that they were armed and responsible for the murder of over 700 members of Syria's security forces in a feature titled, "Syria: The revolution will be weaponised." Despite admitting that hundreds of Syria's security forces died during months of infighting with rebel forces, *Al-Jazeera's* article misrepresented the situation by claiming that, "only now," were protesters thinking about arming themselves and that the Syrian militaries' heavy losses were the result of isolated, armed opposition groups.[29] It is through this purposefully distorted lens that calls for military intervention would continually be made.

After months of denying the existence of insurrectionary elements within the Syrian opposition, the US-based Council on Foreign Relations issued reports confirming that, not only were the "protesters" armed, but that rebel forces on the ground collectively formed a resistance army of 15,000 fighters. The CFR claimed this "Free Syrian Army" was requesting weapons and air support, despite

---

[27] Turkey: US likely to deploy Predator drones, Associated Press, September 24, 2011
[28] Syrian Kurds unite amid onslaught, The Jerusalem Post, September 6, 2011
[29] Syria: The revolution will be weaponised, Al-Jazeera, September 23, 2011

documented reports of weapons being smuggled past Syria's borders from foreign-supporters, most notably, Turkey, Lebanon, Israel, and Libya.[30] CFR's report then goes on to explore the options available to NATO for facilitating "regime change," including the use of "overhead surveillance assets, logistical enablers, peacekeepers, armed drones, combat aircraft, ground troops," and "smuggled weapons." The claims of a large, armed militant force operating inside of Syria directly contradicted the West's concurrent narrative that Syria's military is running rampant and killing defenseless civilians. With an army of "15,000 defectors" attempting to seize the nation by force, with the help of foreign money, weapons, and diplomatic support, one finds it difficult to believe the Syrian government would instead be spending its time conducting massacres. *France24* reported that Syria's Muslim Brotherhood would claim responsibility for two suicide bombings in Damascus that killed 44 people in December 2011, citing an official admission on the group's website:

One of our victorious Sunni brigades was able to target the state security building in Kfar Suseh in the heart of the Omayyad capital Damascus in a successful operation carried out by four of our kamikazes drawn from the best of our glorious men, leaving many dead and wounded from the ranks of the Assad gangs.[31]

In February 2012, both Russia and China exercised their influence in the United Nations Security Council by vetoing a resolution to intervene in Syria on grounds that doing so would comprise Syrian national sovereignty, prompting fiery rhetoric from representatives of the United States. US Ambassador to the United Nations, Susan Rice, called the veto "disgusting and shameful," while US Secretary of State Hillary Clinton lamented, "What happened yesterday at the United Nations was a travesty." The opposition Syrian National Council said it held Moscow and Beijing "responsible for the escalating acts of killing and genocide; it considers this an irresponsible step that is tantamount to a license to kill with impunity." [32] [33]

The diplomatic divergence that had unfolded at the United Nations would lead to the formation of the "Friends of Syria" group, amid calls by former French President Nicolas Sarkozy to form a "group of likeminded nations to coordinate assistance to the Syrian opposition," adding, "France is not giving up." [34] History is a stark reminder of the disingenuous intent of diplomatic support from Paris. Just as the French colonial administration employed the use of foreign soldiers to smother those seeking to abolish the French-mandated protectorate, *Fédération Syrienne,* so too are the French implicated in arming and supporting foreign fighters against Syria. Just as French planes bombed Damascus into submission while former Prime Minister Faris al-Khoury argued the case for Syrian independence before United Nations in 1945, France has again shown its willingness to promote the idea of military intervention, using air superiority to pummel the Assad government. European governments would not be the only political entities to withdraw support from the Syrian government; emerging figures in the Arab world would also

---

[30] Syria: Military Intervention A La Carte, Council on Foreign Relations, November 28, 2011

[31] Thousands join Syrian funeral ceremony, PressTV, December 24, 2012

[32] Russia and China's Syria veto 'disgusting and shameful', says US, The Guardian, February 07, 2012

[33] Syria crisis: Hillary Clinton calls UN veto 'travesty,' BBC, February 05, 2012

[34] Russia and China Block U.N. Action on Crisis in Syria, The New York Times, February 04, 2012

capitulate to Western pressure. Likewise, in Tunisia, the recently installed President Moncef Marzouki (head of the foundation-funded Tunisian League for Human Rights, a recipient of funds directly from the US State Department through the National Endowment for Democracy and George Soros' Open Society Institute) withdrew Tunisia's recognition of the Syrian government, prompting the expulsion of Syrian ambassadors from Tunis and its newly-instated allies in the region.[35]

In Libya, Washington's support for insurgent forces continued unabated, despite a growing census concerned with rouge Islamist elements taking part. In an attempt to address those concerns, US Senator John McCain visited Libya prior to the fall of Gaddafi to address crowds gathered outside Benghazi's historic courthouse and pledged $25 million in foreign assistance to the Libyan opposition, stating:

I have met with these brave fighters, and they are not al-Qaeda. To the contrary: They are Libyan patriots who want to liberate their nation. We should help them do it.[36]

By March 2012, the very same Benghazi courthouse flew the black flags of Al Qaeda.[37] McCain attempted to deceive the world in the pursuit of supporting operatives of US State Department-listed terrorist organizations, militants from the eastern region's Libyan Islamic Fighting Group (LIFG), who fought in both Afghanistan and Iraq against American forces. McCain would not only rhetorically support terrorists, but also provide them with material support including weapons, funds, training, and air support in direct violation of USC § 2339A & 2339B, "providing material support or resources to designated foreign terrorist organizations." McCain's organization, the International Republican Institute (IRI), was mentioned by name in the New York Times for contributing support to opposition elements throughout the Arab world, prior to the events of the "Arab Spring." In an April 2011 article published by the New York Times titled, "U.S. Groups Helped Nurture Arab Uprisings," it was stated:

A number of the groups and individuals directly involved in the revolts and reforms sweeping the region, including the April 6 Youth Movement in Egypt, the Bahrain Center for Human Rights and grass-roots activists like Entsar Qadhi, a youth leader in Yemen, received training and financing from groups like the International Republican Institute, the National Democratic Institute and Freedom House, a nonprofit human rights organization based in Washington.[38]

While officials in Moscow voiced their severe agitation with Washington's refusal to provide legal guarantees that America's anti-ballistic missile system proposed for construction in Eastern Europe would not be used to target Russia, McCain taunted heads of state of in both Russia and China at the height of unrest in North Africa by claiming:

---

[35] Tunisia "to withdraw recognition" of Syria government, Reuters, February 4, 2012
[36] STATEMENT BY SENATOR McCAIN IN BENGHAZI, LIBYA, United States Senator John McCain, April 22, 2011
[37] Benghazi: A Sea of Al-Qaeda Flags, National Review Online, November 05, 2011
[38] U.S. Groups Helped Nurture Arab Uprisings, The New York Times, April 14, 2011

I would be a little less cocky in the Kremlin with my KGB cronies today if I were Vladimir Putin. I would be a little less secure in the seaside resort of President Hu and a few men who govern and decide the fate of 1.3 billion people.[39]

McCain's IRI would be instrumental in generating doubt regarding the validity of Russia's presidential elections by funding several US-backed NGOs, particularly GOLOS, an independent electoral commission seeking to "expose voting irregularities," amid widespread criticism from Russian lawmakers and observer groups. Georgy Fyodorov, chief executive of Russian observer association Civil Control stated:

They have a clear destabilizing tactic; they are carefully conditioning the public to hear some 'breaking' news of election fraud. The media will have a field day taping the ensuing clashes between pro-Kremlin and nationalist youth being dispersed by special police. This kind of footage would dilute any remaining trust in Russian elections. [40]

McCain's role in the attempted destabilization of Russia would pale in comparison to his bellicose rhetoric on Syria, where he has taken every opportunity to call for assisting Syrian opposition fighters by suggesting the use of force against Damascus. McCain would call for US airstrikes on Syria, promoting the use of America's military while being unable to cite any credible or imminent threat to US territorial security, a seemingly punishable offense or, at minimum, a sign of mental instability and grounds for dismissing the ageing Senator. Like McCain, Libya's newly appointed Prime Minister, former Petroleum Institute chairman Abdurrahim el-Keib, would flatly deny allegations by Russian UN Ambassador Vitaly Churkin that Libya was directly funding, training, and arming militants in Syria. El-Keib's denial stands in direct contradiction of reports like the *Telegraph*'s "Leading Libyan Islamist met Syrian Army Opposition Group," where it was reported, "the new Libyan authorities had offered money and weapons to the growing insurgency against Bashar al-Assad." [41] During talks with Libya's el-Keib, US Secretary of State Hillary Clinton would admit that the US was organizing the Syrian opposition into a front similar to what the US and NATO had assembled in Libya before commencing months of NATO bombardment, leading to devastating sieges of the cities of Tripoli, Bani Walid, and Sirte. Clinton would conclude:

Just think, this time last year, the United States was working to build an international coalition of support for the Libyan people, and today, we are proud to continue that support as the people of Libya build a new democracy that will bring about peace and prosperity, and protect the rights and dignity of every citizen.[42]

Clinton's comments would follow widespread reports from Libya indicating that rebels involved in the savage assassination of Muammar Gaddafi were now persecuting migrant workers from Chad and Niger, as well as dark-skinned Libyans in a campaign of racial violence sweeping the country. On a visit to Libya in late August 2011, Former US Congressman Walter Fauntroy claimed to have witnessed

---

[39] McCain: Egypt Revolution Will Have Ripple Effect Across the Globe, FOX News, February 13, 2011
[40] Voters' rights group inciting "Orange Revolution"? RiaNovosti, November 18, 2011
[41] Leading Libyan Islamist met Free Syrian Army opposition group, November 27, 2011
[42] Remarks With Prime Minister Elkeib After Their Meeting, U.S. Department of State, March 8, 2012

French and Danish Special Forces storming small villages late at night, beheading and killing both rebels and loyalists, reports state:

> *The rebels told Fauntroy they had been told by the European forces to stay inside. According to Fauntroy, the European forces would tell the rebels, 'Look at what you did.' In other words, the French and Danish were ordering the bombings and killings, and giving credit to the rebels.*[43]

Following NATO's intervention into Libya, the nation would be plunged into perpetual violence and social division as warring tribes and militias sought to usurp control over territory, thus carving the once unified Libya into a myriad of fiefdoms under the watch of the unstable National Transition Council in Tripoli. BBC's "Libya militia 'terrorises' pro-Gaddafi town of Tawargha," reported that an entire town once populated with 30,000 residents would be abandoned, due to terrorist militias targeting Gaddafi loyalists.[44] In March 2012, disturbing video footage would surface, depicting Arab Libyan rebels force-feeding green Libya flags (representing the period of Gaddafi's rule) to captured African Libyan civilians, while the captors could be heard shouting, "eat your flag, you dog."

Such realities are devoid of Clinton's vision of "rights and dignity for every citizen," a stark precursor to events that would follow in Syria.[45]

By March 16, 2012, *Reuters* would report in their article, "Turkey considers buffer zone along Syria border," that "Turkey is considering setting up a buffer zone inside Syria to tackle a growing flow of refugees fleeing the conflict there." [46] The proposed buffer zone would have indeed been on Syrian soil, requiring an armed Turkish presence to maintain it. Turkey, a nation that has carried out systematic campaigns of violence against the Kurd minority within and beyond its own borders for decades, and still denies the Armenian genocide of the early 1900's, is the least qualified candidate in or around the Middle East to claim "humanitarian concerns" as justification for any geopolitical maneuver. Ankara, with its ambitions of regional hegemony, would continue leading efforts to funnel NATO resources into the hands of militants working to destabilize Syria and overthrow its government. On March 18, 2012, triple suicide bombings targeting government buildings would rip through a Christian neighborhood in the Syrian capital of Damascus, killing an estimated 27 civilians. The *Australian* would report in its article, "Bombs in Syria as Saudis 'send arms to rebels'," that Saudi Arabia (the recipient of significant amounts of military funding from the United States) had begun shipping arms to the Syrian opposition, "Saudi military equipment is on its way to Jordan to arm the Free Syrian Army," quoting an Arab diplomat.[47]

A six-point peace plan crafted by Kofi Annan (a close affiliate of George Soros, Zbigniew Brzezinski, Israeli President Shimon Peres, Egypt's Mohammed ElBaradei, Richard Armitage and Kenneth Adelman) would be put into effect in February 2012, calling for a cease-fire between rebel and government forces.

---

[43] Ex-Congressman Feared Dead in Libya, Returns Home New America Media, September 14, 2011
[44] Libya militia 'terrorises' pro-Gaddafi town of Tawargha, BBC, October 31, 2011
[45] Libyan rebels force black Africans to eat flags in cage, The Telegraph, March 05, 2012
[46] Turkey considers buffer zone along Syria border, ABC, March 17, 2012
[47] Bombs in Syria as Saudis 'send arms to rebels', March 19, 2012

Publications released in March 2012 by The Brookings Institution, a corporate-funded US think-tank noted for influencing American foreign policy, provides further insight into the nature of Washington's objectives in Syria. Brookings' Middle East Memo titled "Saving Syria: Assessing Options for Regime Change," would document admissions that Syria's rebels were cooperating with Al Qaeda and carrying out an increasing amount of sectarian violence, and how Kofi Annan's peace plan would be used in an attempt to establish an occupied "safe haven" on Syrian territory, where further attacks could be launched.[48] Brookings' Memo would meticulously theorize about ways to overthrow the Assad government, including the use of crippling economic sanctions to further incite unrest and the leveraging of human rights abuses to aggressively intervene in Syria:

Working with its Arab, regional, and Western partners, Washington can push for a more effective humanitarian response and pave the way for more aggressive intervention options to topple Assad.

Brookings would attribute heavy budget restraints and a public wary of fighting wars overseas to Washington's strategy of leading from behind, by continually pressuring neighboring countries like Jordan and Turkey to provide support for the militant Syrian opposition:

Israel could posture forces on or near the Golan Heights and, in so doing, might divert regime forces from suppressing the opposition. This posture may conjure fears in the Asad regime of a multi-front war, particularly if Turkey is willing to do the same on its border and if the Syrian opposition is being fed a steady diet of arms and training.

These allies would have to provide secure bases for the opposition on Syria's borders, protected by their own armed forces. Their militaries could do much of the arming and training, in conjunction with the United States. Area intelligence services, perhaps including Israel's, could also work behind the scenes to undermine Asad's regime and bolster the opposition.

The Brookings Memo highlights Washington's commitment to overthrowing the Syrian government using the most cost-effective means possible. While Hillary Clinton and others paid lip service to supporting the ceasefire proposed by the Annan Plan, the report would state in reference to arming the rebels:

Alternatively, the United States might calculate that it is still worthwhile to pin down the Asad regime and bleed it, keeping a regional adversary weak, while avoiding the costs of direct intervention.

The hope is that the United States could fight a 'clean' war from 10,000 feet and leave the dirty work on the ground to the Free Syrian Army, perhaps even obviating a massive commitment to Iraq-style nation-building.

The obscure document released by the Brookings Institution serves as a testament to the underlying politicization of the "Responsibility to Protect" in Syria, as atrocities would be orchestrated as a pretext to protect civilians, to warrant toppling the Syrian government and furthering Washington's geopolitical objectives

---

[48] Saving Syria: Assessing Options for Regime Change, Brookings Institution, March 15, 2012

in the region. As the unrest in Syria continued, it became increasingly more difficult to deny the West's intentional destabilization of Syria by perpetuating extensive bloodshed through radical militant groups operating on Syria's borders, as well as within Syria itself. In late March, Michael E. O'Hanlon, Director of Research and Senior Fellow at Foreign Policy and member of General David Petraeus's External Advisory Board at the Central Intelligence Agency would author an Op-Ed titled, "What Are Our Military Options in Syria?" proposing several contingency options to suit Syria's geopolitical predisposition, as US-backed uprisings, armed militants, and sanctions had all already been set in motion to no avail, leaving only overt military options on the table.[49] The military measures O'Hanlon envisions to achieve the overthrow of Syria's government include:

• **A punitive naval or air operation to encourage a coup against Assad** that would rightfully be considered an outright act of war, designed to completely cut off Syria, including its millions of civilians, from importing or exporting anything. O'Hanlon's article also proposes airstrikes designed to psychologically shake Assad's allies and panic them into defecting and instead, "share power" with the US-backed opposition.

• **A broader Balkans-like campaign to help depose Assad.** By this, O'Hanlon is referring to a campaign similar to that which befell Libya, with the editorial focus on the Balkans, due to its place in historical hindsight and numerous attempts to rewrite its historical outcome as "favorable." Evoking the NATO-led operation that had just unfolded in Libya, complete with the destruction of several major cities, would be a stark reminder to potential defectors in Syria of the cost that comes with allowing a nation to be subjected to NATO-led international intervention. That cost would be the plunging of Syria into perpetual division, instability, violence, and an uncertain political future.

• **The creation of a safe zone for Syrian civilians** bears striking similarity to what Turkey has been elected to create, with such a zone being exploited as a base from which increasing hostilities could be conducted, as suggested by the Brookings Institution, which stated:

An alternative is for diplomatic efforts to focus first on how to end the violence and how to gain humanitarian access, as is being done under Annan's leadership. This may lead to the creation of safe-havens and humanitarian corridors, which would have to be backed by limited military power. This would, of course, fall short of U.S. goals for Syria and could preserve Asad in power. From that starting point, however, it is possible that a broad coalition with the appropriate international mandate could add further coercive action to its efforts.

O'Hanlon indirectly admits that this option may only be accomplished as a result of the successful applications of one or both of the above mentioned options. O'Hanlon did not write these options for the consideration of the Pentagon, but instead, for Western pundits and media outlets that used extortion against Syria's establishment, preying on the fear of Assad's political allies and those across Syria's business community who had stood behind their nation's government. Syria's

---

[49] What Are Our Military Options in Syria?, The New Republic, March 19, 2012

opposition had been entirely dependent on foreign fighters, foreign arms, foreign funds, and an international consensus that allowed such foreign resources to continue flowing to them unabated. While the alternative media reported on abuses committed by the Syrian rebels since the start of the uprising, *Human Rights Watch* (HRW) would issue reports commending the opposition after twelve months of fighting. HRW's March 2012 report titled, "Syria: Armed Opposition Groups Committing Abuses," would detail how Syria's armed opposition conducted a systematic campaign of kidnapping, torture, and mass murder.[50] While the report attempts to focus mainly on atrocities carried out against security forces and government supporters, the mention of civilian victims is made as well. The report states:

Abuses include kidnapping, detention, and torture of security force members, government supporters, and people identified as members of pro-government militias, called shabeeha. Human Rights Watch has also received reports of executions by armed opposition groups of security force members and civilians.

Human Rights Watch also expressed concern about FSA [Free Syrian Army] kidnappings of Iranian nationals, some of whom the group has confirmed are civilians.

HRW's report describes the Syrian opposition's practice of rounding up suspects and killing them without trial, generally on the grounds of confessions coerced through torture. Other executions are simply carried out as reprisals with no apparent offense beyond suspected affiliations being cited. The report indicates that Syria's militant opposition groups, like the NATO-backed rebels in Libya, were lawless, unprincipled, sectarian extremists, who were being marketed as "democracy activists" and "unarmed civilians" in the Western mainstream media. From the early stages of Syria's unrest, the alternative media would cover the tactics of systematic violence used by the opposition, from vandalism and arson, to sniper and bomb attacks and armed insurrectionary campaigns of violence. The findings of (and reactions to) the *Human Rights Watch* report were muted, with most media outlets electing to downplay, spin, or obfuscate the true implications of the war crimes being carried out by Syria's opposition - war crimes which implicated NATO, led by the US, UK, France, and Turkey, as well as their proxy "Arab League," in backing torturers, kidnappers, and mass murderers in their campaign to topple the Syrian government. By early April 2012, the "Friends of Syria" group met in neighboring Turkey to devise a method to rearm and redeploy militant rebel fighters, while demanding Syrian troops be withdrawn from cities recaptured from rebel forces. More specifically, BBC reported in their article titled, "Syria crisis debated at Istanbul talks," that ways were being "explored" to "step up pressure on the Syrian regime and bolster the opposition." The report also makes mention of calls to arm the opposition, and offers to pay salaries to rebel fighters in an effort to entice Syrian military officers to defect.[51] While Moscow and Beijing received harsh criticism and accusations of being complicit with the bloodshed in Syria following their veto at the UNSC, the "Friends of Syria" would openly call for putting pressure on a government

---

[50] Syria: Armed Opposition Groups Committing Abuses, Human Rights Watch, March 20, 2012
[51] Istanbul summit tries to increase pressure on Syria, BBC, April 1, 2012

attempting to restore order across the country, while "bolstering" and arming the opposition.

While allied nations provided funding and supplies to indiscriminate rebel fighters, Western leaders hypocritically claimed the moral high ground by emphasizing their "responsibility to protect" unarmed civilians being killed in the ensuing crossfire. The 2005 UN initiative, the "Responsibility to Protect (R2P)" doctrine follows that if a nation is incapable of providing protection for its own population, it relinquishes its sovereignty to direct intervention by the "international community." Despite the obvious inconsistencies between the alleged narrative and the realities unfolding on the ground in Libya months earlier, NATO evoked the R2P doctrine and began its military intervention to "protect civilians." Far from providing assistance to civilians, NATO provided air support for rebel assaults, intelligence and special operations assistance to rebel military units, and carried out the systematic targeting of Gaddafi's political inner circle, which included bombing the homes of Gaddafi's family, killing his children and his grandchildren in NATO airstrikes.

Allied nations granted diplomatic support to governments led by exiled Libyan politicians and academics, in exchange for lucrative contracts with the new government once Gaddafi's regime was toppled. The United Kingdom budgeted $500 million on NATO's intervention in Libya. However, according to the UK Department of Trade and Investment, contracts to rebuild the nation in areas varying from healthcare and education to electricity and water supplies, were valued at upwards of $300 billion over a 10-year period.[52] Intervention in Libya was made profitable not only by redevelopment contracts, but also by the opportunity to gain greater access to Libya's vast natural resources. Reports issued by the US Office of the Director of National Intelligence warn of an international fresh water deficit by 2030, making Libya's Nubian Sandstone Aquifer System, the world's largest known fossil water aquifer system, a vital and highly strategic dispensary for exerting control over Africa's water reserves.[53] Libya boasts the largest proven oil reserves in Africa and the fifth largest in the world with 76.4 billion barrels as of 2010.[54] The NTC declined business opportunities to countries opposed to NATO's interpretation of its mandate to "protect civilians", countries such as Germany.[55] Several billion dollars worth of construction and arms contracts between Russia and Gaddafi's government were also subject to revaluation.[56] Delegations of the Western-supported National Transition Council met in London to hold talks with top business executives on the "massive opportunity to rebuild Libya," while officials allegedly promised the French oil firm Total up to 35% of all oil contracts in exchange for political support. Eric Denece, director and founder of the French Center for Intelligence Studies, added:

When I was in Libya a few weeks ago, I tried to explain to the NTC that they will have to pay with the money we are going to send them back from the amounts frozen

52 Make money, make war: UK profits from Libya mess, Russia Today, November 11, 2011

53 Global 'water war' threat by 2030 - US intelligence, Russia Today, March 22, 2012

54 BP Statistical Review of World Energy, British Petroleum, June 2011

55 Ruin & Rebuild: Warfare worth $300bln Libya windfall, Russia Today, November 15, 2011

56 Gaddafi demise leads to questions over contracts, Russia Today, October 20, 2011

in the Western banks, they are perfectly conscious of what is going to happen. They are going to give back a lot of money to France, Great Britain and all the senior NATO countries which had been involved in this operation.[57]

Clearly, NATO made a cruel mockery of the "Responsibility to Protect" doctrine, using it to visit catastrophic horrors upon the Libyan people, overturning a unified national government and plunging the entire nation into division and chaos. Despite the failure of NATO's operation in Libya, calls for implementing the R2P model in Syria were made by the allied nations that took part in toppling Gaddafi. From the very beginning of diplomatic efforts to defuse the Syrian crisis, US policy makers admitted that Kofi Annan's "peace mission" in Syria was nothing more than a ruse to preserve NATO's proxy forces from total destruction by creating "safe havens" from which they would operate, prolonging the bloodshed while pressure mounted on the Syrian regime internationally. An April 9th, 2012 posting on NATO's official *"Alliance News Blog"* titled, "US 'already committed to helping Assad fall'," would confirm the United States' commitment to the overthrow of Syria's government, stating that the US is "already committed to helping [President Bashar al-Assad] fall," but is "merely looking for the least violent, lowest cost way to get there." [58]

The article fully disclosed that the US had been equipping the so-called "Free Syrian Army" further admitting that the Kofi Annan brokered "peace deal" was merely a ploy meant to lay the foundation for regime change, stating:

If the pace of the killing slows, that could buy time: time for economic sanctions to undermine the regime, time to cajole Russia to switch sides and help pull the rug out from Assad, but also time for the opposition and its new army to organize themselves into a more effective force.

Compounding their criminality was the fact that, instead of taking advantage of a ceasefire to broker a peace deal and begin reconciliation, NATO officially endorsed using the lull in fighting to prepare the next round of opposition-fueled violence, which they themselves were fully prepared to fund and arm. NATO would admit that military intervention is not a matter of "if" but a matter of "when" depending on a predetermined number of objectives that must be achieved first. These include the Syrian opposition getting better organized, assurances that military aid wouldn't fall into the hands of "radical Islamists," and for Turkey, just as Brookings Institution's documents previously stated, "to establish safe havens for the opposition along its border with Syria."

In late April 2012, Kofi Annan's "peace plan", though publicly endorsed, was fully rejected by both the Syrian rebels and their Western and Arab League backers who would continue openly pledging cash, weapons, and support for rebels who continued fighting. *Reuters* reported in, "UN seeks Syria nod for major aid operation," that the UN was seeking to bring in "aid workers" and open offices all across Syria in order to carry out what they called a "major humanitarian operation." [59] In full violation of the proposed ceasefire, the Western media would instead accuse the

---

[57] 'Libyan oil contracts - not the whole story', Russia Today, September 16, 2011
[58] US 'already committed to helping Assad fall,' Atlantic Council, April 09, 2012
[59] UN seeks Syria nod for major aid operation, Reuters, April 20, 2012

Syrian government of failing to meet its obligations. Neo-Conservative led think tanks like the Henry Jackson Society (HJS), would accuse the Syrian government of "serially violating" the terms of the UN proposed "peace deal." *Al-Jazeera* regular, Michael Weiss of HJS, openly admits that "diplomatic options" were merely being peddled to satisfy public opinion and that ultimately NATO will act unilaterally, outside of the UN, to militarily intervene. As the West continued to fuel the violence and pressure for the approval of "humanitarian access" inside Syria, military intervention would routinely be proposed to combat what will be claimed to be Syrian government "belligerence."

On a nearly daily basis, the Syrian opposition continued carrying out vicious attacks not only on security forces, but a terrorist bombing campaign across Syria that killed and maimed scores of civilians. While the Syrian opposition claimed it lacks the ability to carry out such attacks, its militants would be exposed as very well armed with personnel sheltered in NATO member Turkey, its leadership sheltered in Washington and London, and their fighters wielding not only an endless supply of small arms, but rocket propelled grenades, mortars, missiles, and even tanks. The Syrian government claimed that it had documented a long list of ceasefire violations by the rebels - a list that would be confirmed daily in headlines from across the biased Western media, still attempting to depict the violence as one-sided.

Three months after Iraqi Al Qaeda leader Ayman al-Zawahri called on Muslims from across the Arab World to mobilize and support the Free Syrian Army by encouraging the use of foreign fighters and roadside bombing tactics, *Reuters* would publish an article titled "Outgunned Syria rebels make shift to bombs," which included admissions from the rebels themselves that they were behind the spate of bombings ravaging Syria.[60] [61] Western press and Syrian opposition leaders had previously claimed that these bombings were "false flag" attacks carried out by the Syrian government to undermine the rebels' legitimacy.[62] *Reuters'* article concedes that while the FSA officially is "upholding" the UN truce, its fighters have outright rejected it and are indeed openly in violation of the ceasefire. The report also confirmed Syrian President Bashar al-Assad's statement that his security forces were fighting armed militants - not protesters and civilians - in security operations across Syria before the UN ceasefire came into effect. The reports states:

Since the army routed them from their strongholds in cities, some rebels said they realized that even in guerrilla street battles they could not beat Assad's tanks or artillery. The Syrian Liberation Army's spokesman Qdemati said his group's fighters were now focusing most of their attention on 'manufacturing facilities' for bombs. "You are going to start seeing an escalation as we improve our techniques of bomb-making and delivery."

As the Syrian rebels resorted to indiscriminate terrorist tactics, an explosion in the city of Hama in late April killed 70 people, devastating much of a city block. *Reuters* quoted one rebel fighter as saying, "We are starting to get smarter about

---

[60] Leader of Al Qaeda calls on Muslims to help Syrian rebels, Fox News, February 12, 2012
[61] Outgunned Syria rebels make shift to bombs, Reuters, April 30, 2012
[62] Syrian opposition suspects regime behind bombings, CTV News, March 17, 2012

tactics and use bombs because people are just too poor and we don't have enough rifles, it is just no match for the army, so we are trying to focus on the ways we can fight." *Reuters* attempted to allay the fears of its readers by claiming that the rebels they interviewed insisted that, "unlike al Qaeda, their bombs were aimed at military, and never civilian, targets." Paradoxically, however, the *Reuters* story revealed that the rebel bombing campaign was being carried out by "Sunni insurgents" who learned their bombing skills from fighting US troops in neighboring Iraq - or in other words, the very "al Qaeda" the rebels claim they are not like. A "Syrian Liberation Army" spokesman also admitted that his fighters were operating "manufacturing facilities" for bombs. While the *BBC* originally reported that the Syrian government indiscriminately fired a "SCUD missile" at the city of Hama, reports later surfaced that in fact, the explosion was caused by mishap at a rebel bomb-making facility.[63]

While Syria's rebels have been noted as terrorists, both foreign and domestic, since early 2011 by the alternative media, mainstream media outlets confirmed that Syrian rebels were manufacturing and indiscriminately deploying explosive devices nationwide over a year after the initial reports surfaced. The Western press attempted to obfuscate this fact for as long as possible, irreparably undermining their legitimacy in the process. The UN would begin to admit that indeed, the Syrian rebels were in violation of the ceasefire, only as the violence ran demonstratively rampant and out of control, with arms, funding, equipment, training, and political support for the rebels from the "Friends of Syria" cadre including the US, UK, France, Saudi Arabia, and Qatar.[64] On May 9th, the Brookings Institution predictably declared the Annan "peace deal" a failure and that the time to "stretch" Syria's military to the breaking point through expanded foreign-backed unrest had come. In an article titled, "Annan's Mission Impossible: Why is everyone pretending that the U.N. plan in Syria has a prayer of succeeding?" Brookings' Doha Center director Salman Shaikh depicted the ceasefire's failure as solely the result of the Syrian government's belligerence and brutality, while mentioning nothing of the Syrian opposition's documented, and even admitted, atrocities, stating:

While the international community continues to focus on Annan's efforts, it is unbelievable that Assad and his regime are still not seen as international pariahs. The Syrian government has lied to the international community at every turn. When will the world realize that any attempt to negotiate with Assad is utterly futile? The Assad regime has so far successfully employed a strategy of buying time, agreeing to the Annan plan while doing everything it can to undermine it. Meanwhile, the international community has played into Assad's hands by buying into the fanciful logic that the introduction of unarmed U.N. observers will establish calm inside Syria and moderate the regime's behavior. [65]

And, while portraying the Syrian government as irrationally carrying out a campaign of brutality against the Syrian people, Shaikh admitted that the "Free Syrian Army" was operating militarily out of Turkey and that the Syrian National Council (SNC) represents foreign harbored and influenced leadership. While Shaikh

[63] Syria: Massive explosion in Hama 'kills 70', BBC, April 26, 2012
[64] UN: Both sides in Syria are violating the truce, CBS News, May 1, 2012
[65] Annan's Mission Impossible, Foreign Policy, May 8, 2012

portrayed Syria's minorities as "on the sideline," he declined to explain why they had not joined the foreign-driven unrest. In reality, these minority groups were the hardest hit by rebel atrocities, including Syria's large Christian communities. Christians in Syria have been subjected to what should be described as "ethnic cleansing," not by Syrian security forces, but by NATO-backed death squads under the banner of the "Free Syrian Army." The *Los Angeles Times* reported in their article, "Syria Christians fear life after Assad," how Syria's Christian community fears the emergence of what they describe as "a new dictatorship by the Sunni Muslim majority." [66]

Shaikh's article also revealed another truth with the claim that "opposition leaders inside and outside the country do not have the resources to unite their ranks alone." Surely, any opposition group that represents the vast majority of the Syrian people, as the dominant narrative of the mainstream media claims, would not have trouble finding the resources inside of Syria "alone." Despite Shaikh's insistence to abandon diplomatic attempts to defuse the situation in favor of openly toppling Assad, the unrest in Syria has been undeniably driven by a foreign-backed violent minority and carried out by a combination of violent Sunni-extremists from Syria and many foreign fighters brought in from abroad. Many of Syria's less acknowledged opposition groups, such as the National Coordination Committee, a coalition of left-leaning political parties staunchly opposed to foreign intervention, who represent Syria's internal opposition (as opposed to the Istanbul-based Syrian National Council), find the "Free Syrian Army's" collaboration with foreigners "unacceptable.[67]

By late April 2012, it became clear that NATO and its proxies' efforts to topple the Syrian government were failing, primarily because the movement's semi-covert foreign backing was still not enough to turn the tide. The Brookings Institution called for more overt backing of the Syrian opposition - not excluding foreign military intervention - while the mainstream media continued framing the violence as one-sided when, in reality, the "Free Syrian Army" was conducting a vicious campaign of terrorist violence, even attempting to attack a convoy consisting of Kofi Annan's UN monitors, leaving Syrian security forces with no choice but to continue fighting to restore order.[68] Following the incident, France inexplicably blamed the Syrian government for not providing adequate security to the UN monitors, after a year of condemning the government for attempting to restore order in the face of the very militant violence from which the attacks resulted. A concerted effort was being made by outside forces to sabotage the UN peace plan in every shape, form, and manner, especially through increased violence and particularly in cross-border incidents to help build support for NATO-backed, Turkey-led incursions into Syria to carve out "safe havens." From there, a steady stream of weapons and fighters from around the world would be funneled in, in an attempt to, as Brookings's Shaikh puts it, "stretch" Syria's forces to the breaking point.

---

[66] Syria Christians fear life after Assad, Los Angeles Times, March 7, 2012
[67] "Free Syrian Army's" collaboration with foreigners, RIA Novosti, April 26, 2012
[68] Bomb hits Syrian army truck escorting UN team, Al-Jazeera, May 10, 2012

UN monitors were continually targeted and attacked, narrowly escaping roadside bombs that continued to rock Damascus, as the opposition and media again teamed up to disavow any responsibility. Just as the rebels admitted to *Reuters*, the bombings in Damascus targeted a government intelligence building, the very sort of target the rebels claimed they were looking for. The idealistic comments made to *Reuters* by rebels of "only targeting military forces" fell flat, when Syria's military forces attempted to maintain order in populated civilian areas. Bombs targeting a military convoy or a government building are just as likely to kill and maim civilians, as they are government troops. This is why there are strict, internationally-recognized prohibitions on using improvised explosives, booby-traps, and car bombs off the battlefield and in populated areas - and why people who ignore such prohibitions are called "terrorists." *Reuters* admits that rebels are "channeling" outside donations into "better materials" leading to "more sophisticated bombs," and that the rebels are fighting for a cause "that has widespread support [among] Sunni Arab states and the West." What *Reuters* fails to mention is what support, if any, the rebels have domestically, beyond extremist Sunnis, and how that support will be affected by filling the streets with foreign-funded, indiscriminate terror and carnage.

In early May 2012, the Pentagon itself admitted that Al Qaeda is present in Syria as reports surfaced indicating that foreign fighters, weapons, and cash were flowing over Syria's borders, creating an eruption of violence in northern Lebanon. Indigenous Lebanese factions faced off against each other along sectarian divisions, with initial information indicating that extremist groups backed by the US, Israel, and Saudi Arabia were fighting factions connected to Hezbollah. Extremist leaders across the attempted to frame the violence as "Sunni verses Shi'a," a ploy Hezbollah leader Hassan Nasrallah warned against in 2007 as documented by journalist Seymour Hersh:

> *Nasrallah accused the Bush Administration of working with Israel to deliberately instigate 'fitna,' an Arabic word that is used to mean insurrection and fragmentation within Islam. "In my opinion, there is a huge campaign through the media throughout the world to put each side up against the other," he said. "I believe that all this is being run by American and Israeli intelligence." (He did not provide any specific evidence for this.) He said that the U.S. war in Iraq had increased sectarian tensions, but argued that Hezbollah had tried to prevent them from spreading into Lebanon. (Sunni-Shiite confrontations increased, along with violence, in the weeks after we talked.)* [69]

Violence raged in and around Lebanon's northern port city of Tripoli. While being depicted as chaos "spilling over" from Syria (with both sides identifying as either supporters or opponents of the neighboring Syrian government), it is clear that the violence there was indigenous, sectarian in nature, and directly related to the larger conflict envisioned by Hassan Nasrallah. This prevailing "sectarian" aspect reveals what has been stated by geopolitical analysts since the beginning of unrest in Syria - that the violence was driven not by "pro-democratic" aspirations, but by sectarian violence exploited for the sole purpose of advancing the agenda of foreign meddlers - sectarian violence that has now manifested itself in attacks on Christians, Druze, and

---

[69] The Redirection, The New Yorker, March 5, 2007

Alawites, as well as moderate Sunnis across Syria in the midst of this so-called "democratic revolution."

By May 2012, the involvement of the United States, Saudi Arabia, Qatar, and other Gulf States in supplying weapons, cash, and logistical support to terrorist forces in Syria was further confirmed by the *Washington Post,* in their article, "Syrian rebels get influx of arms with gulf neighbors' money, U.S. coordination." The *Washington Post* not only admitted the involvement of foreign powers provoking unrest in Syria, but confirmed the claims made by Syrian President Bashar al-Assad, that Syria's historically violent Muslim Brotherhood is also directly arming and funding contingents of extremists committing acts of terror across Syria, particularly in areas that had been portrayed as centers of "pro-democracy" protests.[70] These "flashpoints", which had been racked by violence depicted as "repression" by Syrian troops, were now admitted by the Washington Post to be areas where "materiel is being stockpiled." These included the flashpoint city of Idlib on the Turkish-Syrian border, in the suburbs of Damascus, and along Syria's border with Lebanon where weapons, supplies, and cash provided by the US and Saudi Arabia were used to perpetuate the increased violence in Syria in the midst of a ceasefire the West has attempted to disingenuously use to defame the Syrian government. In the midst of a UN ceasefire, the militant Syrian rebel forces continued to do everything possible to hamper the government's ability to restore order, while continuing their campaign with new weapons, in another attempt at violent foreign-backed regime change in areas controlled by Syria's Kurds – a group that had largely remained out of the predominately foreign-backed conflict:

The effect of the new arms appeared evident in Monday's clash between opposition and government forces over control of the rebel-held city of Rastan, near Homs. The Britain-based Syrian Observatory for Human Rights said rebel forces who overran a government base had killed 23 Syrian soldiers.

Paradoxically, the US and Gulf states continued funneling weapons and other forms of material support to the Syrian rebels, even after the Pentagon admitted Al Qaeda presence in Syria.[71] This came after terrorist groups claimed responsibility for a series of bombings that have killed mostly civilians. In the midst of an admitted attempt to increase violence and chaos, the *Washington Post* also declared that NATO-member Turkey would be pressured to invoke Article IV of the NATO Charter, allowing NATO to militarily intervene to "stop" violence that outside forces are openly credited with fomenting. Unlike previous conflicts, the US admission is not a whispered obfuscation of the their intentions, but an open declaration of intent to provoke a war of aggression - a Nuremberg offense for all involved. Here, we see direct parallels between Adolf Hitler's September 1938 campaign of destabilization in Czechoslovakia, and NATO's attempts to destabilize Syria.

The United Nations remained inexplicably silent over revelations that the United States, Saudi Arabia, and other Gulf states, were directly responsible for arming militants in Syria in direct violation of a UN-brokered ceasefire. Additionally, the US

---

[70] Syrian rebels get influx of arms with gulf neighbors' money, U.S. coordination, The Washington Post, May 15, 2012
[71] Al Qaeda's War for Syria, The Wall Street Journal, July 26, 2012

openly threatened to arm Kurdish militants in Syria to "rise up" against the government. While in reality this constitutes a greater threat to neighboring Turkey, and perhaps an attempt to motivate Ankara to take a more aggressive stance against Syria, the threat of purposefully inciting more violence in a conflict that has allegedly claimed "20,000 lives", seems not only grossly irresponsible, but a violation of international peace.[72] As clashes broke out in neighboring Lebanon along the Lebanese-Syrian border, journalist Seymour Hersh exposed a joint US-Israeli-Saudi operation to create a violent Islamist-front and direct it at Hezbollah in Lebanon, President Bashar al-Assad in Syria, and at the Iranian government years earlier. Hersh's 2007 article "The Redirection," would report the fact that these extremist elements, used as proxies by outside forces, had direct ties to Al Qaeda, with many of the militants having either participated in fighting US troops in Iraq and Afghanistan, or affiliations with groups that did:

In 2005, according to a report by the U.S.-based International Crisis Group, Saad Hariri, the Sunni majority leader of the Lebanese parliament and the son of the slain former Prime Minister—Saad inherited more than four billion dollars after his father's assassination—paid forty-eight thousand dollars in bail for four members of an Islamic militant group from Dinniyeh. The men had been arrested while trying to establish an Islamic mini-state in northern Lebanon. The Crisis Group noted that many of the militants had trained in al-Qaeda camps in Afghanistan.

According to the Crisis Group report, Saad Hariri later used his parliamentary majority to obtain amnesty for twenty-two of the Dinniyeh Islamists, as well as for seven militants suspected of plotting to bomb the Italian and Ukrainian embassies in Beirut, the previous year. (He also arranged a pardon for Samir Geagea, a Maronite Christian militia leader, who had been convicted of four political murders, including the assassination, in 1987, of Prime Minister Rashid Karami.) Hariri described his actions to reporters as humanitarian.

In an interview in Beirut, a senior official in the Siniora government acknowledged that there were Sunni jihadists operating inside Lebanon. "We have a liberal attitude that allows Al Qaeda types to have a presence here," he said. He related this to concerns that Iran or Syria might decide to turn Lebanon into a "theatre of conflict."

Saad Hariri, former prime minister of Lebanon, is admittedly a co-conspirator in US-Israeli-Saudi designs to destabilize with militant extremists and violently overthrow the Syrian government. While Hariri feigns anti-Israeli sentiment and makes public calls for Lebanese to refrain from sectarian violence, he was the primary facilitator of extremists crossing over into Syria, and their creating chaos in the streets of Lebanon. A 2010 report issued by the Fortune 500-funded International Crisis Group describes in detail Hariri's deep ties, and indeed dependence, on the West.[73] The report also made mention of extensive US funding behind Hariri's faction, then led by Fouad Siniora, augmenting the creation of militant forces:

---

[72] Syria death toll hits 20,000: NGO, Financial Review, July 29, 2012
[73] Lebanon's Politics: The Sunni Community and Hariri's Future Current, International Crisis Group, May 26, 2010

The United States has also given clandestine support to the Siniora government, according to the former senior intelligence official and the U.S. government consultant. "We are in a program to enhance the Sunni capability to resist Shiite influence, and we're spreading the money around as much as we can," the former senior intelligence official said. The problem was that such money 'always gets in more pockets than you think it will,' he said. "In this process, we're financing a lot of bad guys with some serious potential unintended consequences. We don't have the ability to determine and get pay vouchers signed by the people we like and avoid the people we don't like. It's a very high-risk venture."

American, European, and Arab officials I spoke to told me that the Siniora government and its allies had allowed some aid to end up in the hands of emerging Sunni radical groups in northern Lebanon, the Bekaa Valley, and around Palestinian refugee camps in the south. These groups, though small, are seen as a buffer to Hezbollah; at the same time, their ideological ties are with Al Qaeda.

CNN reported that "anti-Assad clerics" have been shot by Lebanese soldiers" and, just as was seen during the assassination of Rafic Hariri, demagogues and outside forces attempted to draw Sunni Muslims into a conflict with Shi'as.[74] A strategy of tension was used to divide the Lebanese people into a deadly conflict mirroring the sectarian, not "democracy," driven unrest ravaging Syria. With Saad Hariri, the US, and Saudi Arabia overtly working to undermine Syrian stability, it appears that all of the designs described by Seymour Hersh in 2007 were now coming to fruition. Western media's reportage of violence in Lebanon would create a disingenuous depiction of it being "spilt over" from Syria, meant to portray a general sense of chaos consuming the region. In actuality, it is a premeditated destabilization dependent on fostering violence between Sunni and Shi'a Muslims, just as was purposefully done in Iraq to balk an effective Sunni-Shi'a alliance that achieved initial success fighting a foreign occupation led by the US starting in 2003. Hariri portends that his alliance with the US, Israel, and the Saudis is simply an attempt to protect "Sunnis" from a "Shi'a threat." As empires have done all throughout history, Hariri's invitation from the West to meddle in his own nation's affairs has opened the door to the destruction and dismemberment of not only his enemies, but inevitably his own movement as well.

Despite a current UN ceasefire the West has continuously berated the Syrian government for violating, reports issued by corporate think tanks such as the Brookings' Institute have continually called for using the ceasefire to reorganize and rearm terrorist proxies. As a consequence of that policy, the next round of destructive violence in Syria shook and disturbed the world. On May 25, 2012, 108 people were brutally murdered, including 34 women and 49 children in two opposition-controlled villages in the Houla district, northwest of Homs. The victims showed signs of being killed at close range, while many had their throats slit and showed signs of being executed at point-blank range. While the Syrian government reported that al-Qaeda terrorist groups were responsible for the killings in an

---

[74] Soldiers shoot anti-Assad clerics in Lebanon, triggering fresh violence, CNN, May 21, 2012

attempt to subvert the peace plan, UN investigators proposed that government-hired Alawite militias known as "Shabiha" were responsible for the killing.

Initial reports issued by Western media organizations had claimed that Syrian government shelling was responsible for the 90 "confirmed" deaths by UN monitors who later arrived on the scene. However, conflicting reports from across Gulf State media claim the deaths, particularly those of children, were caused by "knives" and other short-range weapons. Images broadcasted by both the opposition and the Syrian government's SANA News network showed slain families laying dead within intact structures, the result of a combination of brutality including close range small arms fire and bladed weapons as claimed by Gulf State networks.[75] SANA News argues that terrorist groups committed the atrocities, as it consistently maintained throughout the duration of the unrest. The West and its allies however, have presented conflicting, and ever-shifting narratives to obfuscate the increasingly depraved atrocities committed by their own proxy rebel forces.

Former British intelligence officer Alastair Crooke commented on the nature of the attacks, and how they were not characteristic of the cultural region to which Syria belongs, suggesting that the massacre had its tactical and ideological roots in the Iraq war:

This type of killing, beheadings, slitting of throats (of children too), and of this mutilation of bodies, has been a characteristic not of Levantine Islam, not of Syria, not of Lebanon, but what happened in the Anbar province of Iraq. And so it seems to point very much in the direction of groups that have been associated with the war in Iraq against the United States who have perhaps returned to Syria, or perhaps Iraqis who have come up from Anbar to take part in it. I think the attack is more close to Musab al-Zarqawi [who declared an all out war on Shia in Iraq], than al-Qaeda as we know it, in the sense that Zarqawi and Iraq gave birth to this very strong, bigoted, anti-Shia, anti-Iranian rhetoric. Much of that came into Syria when fighters from Anbar returned to their homes around Homs and Hama. So yes, we're talking about al-Qaeda like groups that are at the very end of the spectrum of the opposition. They may be a minority in terms of the numbers of the overall opposition, but they are defining the war.[76]

Before UN monitors even arrived in Houla, the US, UK, and France were already calling for the "international community" to move against the Syrian government. Western mainstream media sources reported that militant extremists, material assistance and high-end weapons had been freely flowing for months in the Houla region, close to the nearby Lebanese border. French Foreign Minister Laurent Fabius urged for more support to be given to the Syrian opposition, who were now long exposed as employing terrorist tactics, including indiscriminate bombings and, according to both the UN and *Human Rights Watch*, the kidnapping, torture, and murder of civilians.[77] Almost immediately after UN monitors arrived in Houla, Syria, the so-called "Free Syrian Army" officially declared that it would abandon the UN peace plan, as predicted by Western think-tanks such as the Brookings Institution,

---

[75] New Massacres by al-Qaeda-linked Terrorist Groups against Families in al-Shumariyeh and Taldo in Homs Countryside, SANA News, May 26, 2012

[76] Pointblank massacre: Massive fallout from Houla killings, Russia Today, May 29, 2012

[77] France, U.K. Urge Support for Syrian Opposition, Bloomberg, May 26, 2012

who called for the ending of the UN "ceasefire" and the recommencing of violence to overthrow the Syrian government. UK Foreign Office minister Alistair Burt would state:

We are appalled at what appears to be credible reports that the Syrian regime has been responsible for the deaths of 92 civilians in Houla, including 32 children. The UN Head of Mission has been able to confirm the numbers and also that artillery tank shells have been used. If this is the case then it's an act of pure, naked savagery and we condemn it in the most strongest possible terms.[78]

Events in Houla lead Western states to expel Syrian diplomats and on June 1st, the United Nations Human Rights Council voted to condemn Syria, calling for an international criminal inquiry into the events. Western media has largely relied on unconfirmed opposition accounts crediting Shabiha pro-government Alawite militias with carrying out massacres across Syria as a result of the Assad government "brainwashing the militia into believing the Sunni majority was their enemy," as reported by The Telegraph In early June.[79] During a speech in the Syrian parliament, Assad called the attacks in Houla "abominable," stating:

This crisis is not an internal crisis. It is an external war carried out by internal elements, if we work together; I confirm that the end to this situation is near. What happened in Houla... and what we described as ugly and abominable massacres, or true monstrosities - even monsters do not perpetrate what we have seen. We are not facing a political problem because if we were, this party would put forth a political program. What we are facing is an attempt to sow sectarian strife and the tool of this is terrorism, the issue is terrorism. We are facing a real war waged from the outside, and will continue firmly confronting terrorism, leaving the door open for those who want to return. I urge those who are still hesitant to do so, to take this step. The state will not take revenge.[80]

Rainer Hermann, a Middle East correspondent of the German newspaper *Frankfurter Allgemeine Zeitung* published an alternative account of the events in Houla, alleging that extremist anti-Assad Sunni militants carried out the massacre, targeting pro-government Alawi and Shia minorities stating:

After Friday prayers on May 25 more than 700 gunmen organized in three groups under the leadership of Abdurrazzaq Tlass and Yahya Yusuf, coming from Rastan, Kafr Laha and Akraba, and attacked three army checkpoints near Taldou. The rebels, who were superior in numbers, and the (mostly also Sunni) soldiers fought a bloody battle in which two dozen soldiers, most of them conscripts, were killed. During and after the fighting, rebels supported by residents of Taldou wiped out the entire families of Sayyid and Abdarrazzaq. They had refused to join the opposition. Those killed were almost exclusively from families belonging to Houla's Alawi and Shia minorities. Over 90% of Houla's population is Sunni. Several dozen members of a family were slaughtered, which had converted from Sunni to Shia Islam. Members of the Shomaliya, an Alawi family, were also killed, as was the family of a Sunni member of the Syrian parliament

---

[78] UK condemns 'pure naked savagery' of Houla killings, The Telegraph, May 27, 2012
[79] The Shabiha: Inside Assad's death squads, The Telegraph, June 02, 2012
[80] Assad says Houla killings monstrous, sees end to crisis, Reuters, June 3, 2012

who is regarded as a collaborator. Immediately following the massacre, the perpetrators are supposed to have filmed their victims and then presented them as Sunni victims in videos posted on the internet.[81]

The report issued by *Frankfurter Allgemeine Zeitung* is entirely plausible, considering that the *Human Rights Watch* report on Syria's opposition documented the outstanding cases of violence conducted largely on sectarian grounds, motivated by anti-Shi'a and anti-Alawite sentiments, with cited abuses committed by militant Salafist groups and members of the opposition Free Syrian Army. Although UN observers admitted they were unable to determine the perpetrators of the Houla massacre with no firm evidence to inculpate the Syrian government, UN chief Ban Ki-moon declared that the Assad government had lost its legitimacy, channeling calls by President Barak Obama, US Secretary of State Hillary Clinton and British Prime Minister David Cameron for Assad to step down. Western nations continued moving ahead with their calls for "action" against the Assad regime and continued to condemn the Syrian government, which according to the activists they are allegedly citing, were not even responsible for the massacre. In late July 2012, reports issued by the German Federal Intelligence Service (BND) confirmed that al Qaeda has carried out "about 90 terrorist attacks" in Syria between late December 2011 and early July 2012, including involvement in the May 25th Houla massacre.[82] Reports of killings were framed to fit a pre-determined conclusion, in line with the foreign policy objectives of Western capitals by implicating the Assad regime in orchestrating violence in order to build popular support for aggressively toppling the Syrian government.

Russian Foreign Minister Sergey Lavrov has recently accused external forces of inciting violence by providing arms and material assistance to militant opposition forces, stating, "They want the international community to be filled with indignation and start a full-blown intervention in Syria." [83] Following the killings, US Treasury Secretary Timothy Geithner called on the world to exert "maximum financial pressure" on Assad's government through strong sanctions that "can help hasten the day the Assad regime relinquishes power," while assuring that the US would support the use of force against Syria as authorized under Chapter 7 of the United Nations charter.[84] One can only imagine the international outcry should the Syrian government have declared it was abandoning the UN-brokered "cease-fire" and resolved to dealing with its opponents in the "only language they understand, violence" – as stated by representatives of the Free Syrian Army. However, the Syrian government did not abandon the ceasefire, and would continue to host hundreds of UN monitors. Instead, it was the opposition making such claims - claims that would continually go unchallenged by the so-called "international community."

The events of Houla could be compared to what unfolded in the summer of 1939, when the Nazi forces, eager to portray themselves as hapless victims to justify acts of

---

[81] Abermals Massaker in Syrien, Frankfurter Allgemeine Zeitung, June 07, 2012

[82] German intel.: Qaeda behind terror in Syria, PressTV, July 26, 2012

[83] Annan plan 'only chance for peace' but stalled by intervention supporters - Lavrov, Russia Today, June 09, 2012

[84] Geithner warns Syria of UN action, as Clinton heads to Istanbul to talk strategy with allies, 570 News, June 06, 2012

military aggression, staged a border incident intended to falsely implicate neighboring Poland. After staging border incidents involving German troops attacking their own radio station to frame Poland for unwarranted aggression, Hitler ordered the Nazi invasion of Poland. Ironically enough, it is the United States' own Holocaust Memorial Museum that not only gives us an account of these events, but an entire lesson regarding "Deceiving the Public:"

Throughout the Second World War, Nazi propagandists disguised military aggression aimed at territorial conquest as righteous and necessary acts of self-defense. They cast Germany as a victim or potential victim of foreign aggressors, as a peace-loving nation forced to take up arms to protect its populace or defend European civilization against Communism. The war aims professed at each stage of the hostilities almost always disguised actual Nazi intentions of territorial expansion and racial warfare. This was propaganda of deception, designed to fool or misdirect the populations in Germany, German-occupied lands, and the neutral countries.

In summer of 1939, as Hitler and his aides finalized plans for the invasion of Poland, the public mood in Germany was tense and fearful. Germans were emboldened by the recent dramatic extension of Germany's borders into neighboring Austria and Czechoslovakia without having fired a shot; but they did not line the streets calling for war, as the generation of 1914 had done. Before the German attack on Poland on September 1, 1939, the Nazi regime launched an aggressive media campaign to build public support for a war that few Germans desired. To present the invasion as a morally justifiable, defensive action, the German press played up "Polish atrocities," referring to real or alleged discrimination and physical violence directed against ethnic Germans residing in Poland. Deploring Polish 'warmongering' and 'chauvinism,' the press also attacked the British for encouraging war by promising to defend Poland in the event of German invasion.

The Nazi regime even staged a border incident designed to make it appear that Poland initiated hostilities with Germany. On August 31, 1939, SS men dressed in Polish army uniforms 'attacked' a German radio station at Gleiwitz (Gliwice). The next day, Hitler announced to the German nation and the world his decision to send troops into Poland in response to Polish 'incursions' into the Reich. The Nazi Party Reich Press Office instructed the press to avoid the use of the word 'war'. They were to report that German troops had simply beaten back Polish attacks, a tactic designed to define Germany as the victim of aggression. The onus of responsibility for declaring war would be left to the British and French.[85]

From Venezuela to Thailand, Western-backed opposition groups have historically been found to trigger unrest, and use it as cover to assassinate civilians and members of their own movements, only to then blame it on the targeted government in order to exacerbate the conflict until a critical mass is reached and that government is toppled. The Houla massacre shares identical characteristics with other engineered atrocities around the world, simply on a larger scale, involving militants most likely not affiliated with local FSA fighters or the Syrian government, but foreign elements just as the Syrian government has claimed.

---

[85] Deceiving the Public, United States Holocaust Memorial Museum, May 11, 2011

38 *Subverting Syria*

In a disturbing prelude to the sectarian extremism sown in Syria, Journalist Trish Schuh would interview Ziad Abdel Nour, in 2005. Nour, a corporate-financier and founder of "Blackhawk Partners" as well as chairman of the Neo-Conservative run "United States Committee for a Free Lebanon," has consorted with fellow committee members including Morris Amitay of the Jewish Institute for National Security Affairs, Michael Rubin of the American Enterprise Institute, and PNAC signatories Paula Dobriansky, James Woolsey, Frank Gaffney, and Daniel Pipes, for years to foment the very bloodshed, instability and atrocities that have unfolded in Syria:

Both the Syrian and Lebanese regimes will be changed- whether they like it or not- whether it's going to be a military coup or something else... and we are working on it. We know already exactly who's going to be the replacements. We're working on it with the Bush administration.

These guys who came to power, who rule by power, can only be removed by power. This is Machiavelli's power game. That's how it is. This is how geopolitics — the war games, power games — work. I know inside out how it works, because I come from a family of politicians for the last 60 years. Look, I have access to the top classified information from the CIA from all over the world. They call me, I advise them. I know exactly what's going on. And this will happen.

This Bashar Al Assad-Emil Lahoud regime is going to go whether it's true or not. When we went to Iraq whether there were weapons of mass destruction or not, the key is — we won. And Saddam is out! Whatever we want, will happen. Iran? We will not let Iran become a nuclear power. We'll find a way; we'll find an excuse - to get rid of Iran. And I don't care what the excuse is. There is no room for rogue states in the world. Whether we lie about it, or invent something, or we don't... I don't care. The end justifies the means. What's right? Might is right, might is right. That's it. Might is right.

So Saddam wanted to prove to the whole world he was strong? Well, we're stronger- he's out! He's finished. And Iran's going to be finished and every single Arab regime that's like this will be finished. Because there is no room for us capitalists and multi-nationalists in the world to operate with regimes like this. It's all about money. And power. And wealth... and democracy has to be spread around the world. Those who want to espouse globalization are going to make a lot of money, be happy, their families will be happy. And those who aren't going to play this game are going to be crushed, whether they like it or not! [86]

Schuh's interview with Abdel Nour profiles a criminal mind not only psychologically and operationally capable of engineering an event such as the Houla massacre, but a mind who possessed the intent and motive to do so. Nour's disturbing display of megalomania dovetails with the *New Yorker*'s 2007 article, "The Redirection," written by journalist Seymour Hersh, which documents how the United States, Israel, and Saudi Arabia, along with Abdel Nour's Hariri faction in Lebanon, were preparing a regional army of sectarian extremists to destabilize the Shi'a-led authorities & administrations of the Middle East. Hersh's report included an interview with former-CIA agent Robert Baer in Lebanon who warned of the need to protect Christians from a predictable onslaught by US-Israeli-Saudi-backed sectarian

[86] Faking the Case Against Syria, Counterpunch, November 18, 2005

extremists - an onslaught that would play out against Syria's 10 percent Christian population. Not only did US, Israeli, and Saudi conspirators purposely unleash sectarian extremists inside of Syria - they did so with the full knowledge that atrocities like the one in Houla, Syria would inevitably result.

For decades, every nation across the Arab World, from Algeria to Morocco, Egypt to Syria, have fought against sectarian extremists from organizations like the Muslim Brotherhood and Al Qaeda. Algeria, for example, fought arduously against violent extremists attempting to overrun their secular society and target ethnic and religious minorities including Christians and even Sunni moderates – this period has come to be referred to as the "lost" or "black decade." Algeria faced amongst others, Al Qaeda in the Islamic Maghreb (AQIM), a US State Department-listed terrorist organization linked directly to neighboring Libya's "Libyan Islamic Fighting Group" (LIFG) which was armed, trained, funded, and politically backed by NATO to overrun Muammar Gaddafi. In both Egypt and Syria, it was the Muslim Brotherhood that had attempted to overrun secular governments with violence, mirroring exactly what has unfolded during the Syrian uprising. Today, the Western press decries Egyptian and Syrian efforts to hem in these sectarian extremists, particularly in Syria where the government is accused of "massacring" armed Brotherhood militants in Hama in 1982. The constitutions of secular Arab nations across Northern Africa and the Middle East, including the newly rewritten Syrian Constitution, have attempted to exclude sectarian political parties, especially those with "regional" affiliations to prevent the Muslim Brotherhood and Al Qaeda affiliated political movements from ever coming back to power.[87]

The Syrian referendum for its new constitution, as well as elections held under this new constitution, would be boycotted by the so-called "Free Syrian Army" and its political wing, specifically because they are sectarian extremists with regional affiliations. The West would back these boycotts, calling the Syrian reforms "laughable." Since at least 2007, the West, particularly the US, along with Israel and Saudi Arabia, attempted to build up both the Muslim Brotherhood and smaller, armed extremist groups with direct ties to Al Qaeda, in order to directly target Lebanon, Syria, and Iran. Begun under the Bush administration and continuing seamlessly under Obama, the Muslim Brotherhood was already described as being backed by the US and Israel, who were funneling support through the Saudis so as to not compromise the "credibility" of the so-called "Islamic" movement. Journalist Seymour Hersh reported that members of the Lebanese Saad Hariri clique, then led by Fouad Siniora, had been the go-between for US planners and the Syrian Muslim Brotherhood. Hersh reported that a supporter of the Lebanese Hariri faction had met Dick Cheney in Washington and relayed personally the importance of using the Muslim Brotherhood in Syria in any move against the ruling government:

[Walid] Jumblatt then told me that he had met with Vice-President Cheney in Washington last fall to discuss, among other issues, the possibility of undermining Assad. He and his colleagues advised Cheney that, if the United States does try to move

---

87 Syrian elections branded 'a sham,' BBC, May 04, 2012

against Syria, members of the Syrian Muslim Brotherhood would be "the ones to talk to," Jumblatt said.

There is evidence that the Administration's redirection strategy has already benefitted the Brotherhood. The Syrian National Salvation Front is a coalition of opposition groups whose principal members are a faction led by Abdul Halim Khaddam, a former Syrian Vice-President who defected in 2005, and the Brotherhood. A former high-ranking C.I.A. officer told me, "The Americans have provided both political and financial support. The Saudis are taking the lead with financial support, but there is American involvement." He said that Khaddam, who now lives in Paris, was getting money from Saudi Arabia, with the knowledge of the White House. (In 2005, a delegation of the Front's members met with officials from the National Security Council, according to press reports.) A former White House official told me that the Saudis had provided members of the Front with travel documents.

In May 2012, outlets such as *Reuters* reported that the Syrian arm of the Muslim Brotherhood has been leading the US, Israeli, and Saudi-backed sectarian violence that has been ravaging Syria for over a year:

Working quietly, the Brotherhood has been financing Free Syrian Army defectors based in Turkey and channeling money and supplies to Syria, reviving their base among small Sunni farmers and middle class Syrians, opposition sources say.[88]

A June 5th 2012 *Bloomberg* op-ed titled, "Annan Should Talk to Putin, Not Assad, to Fix Syria," attempted to indict Moscow and Beijing in sharing the blame for the carnage seen in the Houla Massacre. The article conceded that the violence in Syria is sectarian.[89] The words "democracy" and "freedom," that had been disingenuously used since the beginning of the "Arab Spring," would be dropped altogether as the Western press threw its full weight behind the long-planned sectarian war that the US, Israel, and Saudi Arabia have been cultivating for years:

What Houla indicates is that the sectarian civil war between Syria's Sunnis and Alawites that the world had long feared has begun. Assad's claim in a speech June 3 that terrorists conducted the slaughter of fellow Sunnis to create an international outcry is laughable. Any evidence there is suggests that the Alawite Shabiha militia, working in tandem with the government military, was responsible.

While some members of the Syrian government's security forces may have used excessive force when battling opposition fighters in residential neighborhoods, leading to unintended civilian deaths, it is under the government of Bashar al-Assad that Syria's large populations of ethnic and religious minorities, particularly Shi'a Muslims, moderate Sunnis, Christians, and Druze have been protected from sectarian onslaught perpetuated by extremists and rebel fighters cultivated by the West. Journalist Seymour Hersh's 2007 article "The Redirection," would foreshadow the very "sectarian civil war" that *Bloomberg* openly insinuated:

Robert Baer, a former longtime C.I.A. agent in Lebanon, has been a severe critic of Hezbollah and has warned of its links to Iranian-sponsored terrorism. But now, he told

---

[88] Syria's Muslim Brotherhood rise from the ashes, Reuters, May 06, 2012
[89] Annan Should Talk to Putin, Not Assad, to Fix Syria, Bloomberg, June 04, 2012

me, *"we've got Sunni Arabs preparing for cataclysmic conflict, and we will need somebody to protect the Christians in Lebanon. It used to be the French and the United States who would do it, and now it's going to be Nasrallah and the Shiites."*

Bloomberg concluded that Russia must withdraw support for the Syrian government, which has demonstrably worked to protect both Syria's secular society as well as its vast populations of ethnic and religious minorities, in order to avert further bloodshed. Clearly, just as Russia withdrew support from the Gaddafi regime in Libya under former President Dmitry Medvedev, Russia's withdrawal of support from the Syrian government under President Vladimir Putin would not mark the end of violence. Instead, it would merely mark the end of contested violence and the beginning of unchecked lawlessness, atrocities and widespread killing by sectarian extremists flush with Western cash, weapons, and political support.

In early June 2012, members of Syria's Christian community began accusing the Free Syrian Army of waging a sectarian war on Syria's religious minorities. *Agenzia Fides*, an online information service for International Pontifical Mission Societies would accurately corroborate events on the ground by reporting the testimony of Syria-based French Bishop Philip Tournyol Clos, stating:

The picture for us is utter desolation: the church of Mar Elian is half destroyed and that of Our Lady of Peace is still occupied by the rebels. Christian homes are severely damaged due to the fighting and completely emptied of their inhabitants, who fled without taking anything. The area of Hamidieh is still shelter to armed groups independent of each other, heavily armed and bankrolled by Qatar and Saudi Arabia. All Christians (138,000) have fled to Damascus and Lebanon, while others took refuge in the surrounding countryside. The enemies of Syria have enlisted some of the Muslim Brotherhood in order to destroy the brotherly relations that traditionally existed between Muslims and Christians: Yet, to date, they are not able to: they have provoked a contrary reaction and the two communities are more united than before. The Syrian soldiers in fact, continue to face foreign fighters, mercenaries Libyans, Lebanese militants from the Gulf, Afghans, Turks.[90]

On June 7th 2012, US Ambassador to the UN Susan Rice declared that the West was prepared to "take actions outside of the Annan plan and the authority of this [UN security] council," to implement regime change in Syria in response to the Houla massacre.[91] Russian Foreign Minister Sergey Lavrov repeated that his nation opposes any attempt to intervene or level sanctions against Syria, accusing the West of purposefully perpetuating violence in order to sabotage peace efforts and create a pretense for NATO-enforced regime change Lavrov warned that "the way the Syrian crisis is resolved will play an important role in the world tomorrow; whether the world will be based on the UN charter, or a place where might makes right." Lavrov's sentiments were echoed by China, Iran, and South America's ALBA nations, whose collective populations equate to over 1.5 billion people. Lavrov would make statements during a live press conference, focusing on evidence contradicting the politically motivated coverage of Syria's conflict by the Western media. Lavrov

---

[90] The desolation of Homs and the war of information ": the words of a greek-catholic Archimandrite, Agenzia Fides, June 04, 2012
[91] US ready to act on Syria outside UN? Russia Today, May 31, 2012

elaborated Russia's stance by saying it would accept Syrian President Bashar al-Assad stepping down if, and only if, unconditional negotiations began, and both sides could come to an agreement independent of foreign influence.

On June 10th, 2012, *Russia Today* issued a report titled, "Syrian rebels aim to use chemical weapons, blame Damascus," warning of a possible plot being fomented by Syrian rebels inside NATO member Turkey.[92] The plot involves Syrian rebels deploying chemical weapons obtained in Libya against Syrian civilians, then blaming the Syrian government for the mass casualty event. This, of course, would provide the West the "casus belli" it has been searching for to circumvent the UN Security Council and implement its long-planned campaign of regime change. As a consequence of NATO's operation in Libya, much of Gaddafi's arsenal of military weaponry had reportedly fallen into the hands of rebel fighters. Since then, Libya's militants, led by commanders of Al Qaeda's Libyan Islamic Fighting Group (LIFG), have armed sectarian extremists across the Arab World, from as far West as Mali, to as far East as Syria. Additionally, as a result of NATO's intervention in Libya, the scattered military's extensive arsenal of anti-aircraft missiles has also fallen into the hands of Libyan militants, to then be proliferated throughout LIFG's network of affiliates - all of which are sectarian extremists, many with direct ties to Al Qaeda. The *Washington Post* in their article, "Libyan missiles on the loose," reported:

Two former CIA counterterrorism officers told me last week that technicians recently refurbished 800 of these man-portable air-defense systems (known as MANPADS) — some for an African jihadist group called Boko Haram that is often seen as an ally of al-Qaeda — for possible use against commercial jets flying into Niger, Chad and perhaps Nigeria.[93]

More than any other nation, the United States has been adept at deploying nuclear, biological, and chemical weapons of mass destruction against their enemies - from nuclear bombs upon Japan, to depleted uranium and white phosphorus upon Iraq, to Agent Orange all across Vietnam. It stands to reason then, that these weapons would eventually end up in the hands of the their proxies as well. For an opposition so transparently dishonest, which has already been caught attempting to frame the Syrian government for mass-casualty events and atrocities of their own doing, it is at least plausible that militant rebel groups with the insidious motivations to use them against civilian populations could also be capable of deploying weapons of mass destruction that are more than within their means of obtaining. On June 17th, 2012, the US was caught lying, regarding Russian gunships being shipped to Syria. In the *New York Times*' "Copters in Syria May Not Be New, U.S. Officials Say," a senior defense department official admitted that, when US Secretary of State Hillary Clinton made her fraudulent claim regarding Russian weapon shipments, she "put a little spin on it to put the Russians in a difficult position." The *New York Times* continued by stating, "Mrs. Clinton's claim about the helicopters, administration officials said, is part of a calculated effort to raise the pressure on Russia to abandon President Bashar al-Assad, its main ally in the Middle East." This blatant act of deception and disinformation is indicative of the campaign of fabrication

---

[92] Syrian rebels aim to use chemical weapons, blame Damascus – report, Russia Today, June 10, 2012
[93] Libyan missiles on the loose, The Washington Post, May 9, 2012

orchestrated by the US State Department, the British Foreign Office, and Western and Gulf State news outlets around the world to demonize both the Syrian government and its extensive allies around the world.[94]

On June 21, 2012, The *New York Times* confirmed what alternative media outlets and numerous geopolitical analysts had been reporting since the first months of the uprising in 2011, that outside forces, including the American CIA, were supplying Syria's rebels with weapons and material assistance from Southern Turkey. In "C.I.A. Said to Aid in Steering Arms to Syrian Opposition," the *New York Times* stated:

A small number of C.I.A. officers are operating secretly in southern Turkey, helping allies decide which Syrian opposition fighters across the border will receive arms to fight the Syrian government, according to American officials and Arab intelligence officers. The weapons, including automatic rifles, rocket-propelled grenades, ammunition and some antitank weapons, are being funneled mostly across the Turkish border by way of a shadowy network of intermediaries including Syria's Muslim Brotherhood and paid for by Turkey, Saudi Arabia and Qatar, the officials said. The C.I.A. officers have been in southern Turkey for several weeks, in part to help keep weapons out of the hands of fighters allied with Al Qaeda or other terrorist groups, one senior American official said. The Obama administration has said it is not providing arms to the rebels, but it has also acknowledged that Syria's neighbors would do so. By helping to vet rebel groups, American intelligence operatives in Turkey hope to learn more about a growing, changing opposition network inside of Syria and to establish new ties. 'C.I.A. officers are there and they are trying to make new sources and recruit people,' said one Arab intelligence official who is briefed regularly by American counterparts. American officials and retired C.I.A. officials said the administration was also weighing additional assistance to rebels, like providing satellite imagery and other detailed intelligence on Syrian troop locations and movements. The administration is also considering whether to help the opposition set up a rudimentary intelligence service. But no decisions have been made on those measures or even more aggressive steps, like sending C.I.A. officers into Syria itself, they said.[95]

Undeniably, the West, led by the US and its Gulf State proxies, had been arming terrorists, particularly the Muslim Brotherhood, while berating the Syrian government for "violating" a UN-mandated ceasefire and for "failing to protect" its population. The Muslim Brotherhood has been combated by nations across the Arab World to stem the tide of their sectarian extremism, violence, and their targeted erosion of secular nation-states. Ironically, the US, which has claimed to be fighting the forces of sectarian extremism and "terrorism" for over a decade, has been revealed as the primary enabler of the most violent and extreme terrorist organizations in the world. These include, in addition to the Muslim Brotherhood, the Libyan Islamic Fighting Group (LIFG) in Libya, Baloch terrorists in Pakistan, and the Mujahideen-e-Khalq (MEK) currently based in Iraq and being used as proxies against Iran. Efforts to impose an arms embargo on Syria is now revealed to be one-sided, aimed at giving rebels an advantage in the prolonged bloodbath with the

---

[94] Copters in Syria May Not Be New, U.S. Officials Say, The New York Times, June 13, 2012
[95] C.I.A. Said to Aid in Steering Arms to Syrian Opposition, The New York Times, June 21, 2012

intent of tipping the balance in favor of Western proxy-forces, rather than ending the violence as soon as possible as claimed by the UN, and in particular, Kofi Annan.

Despite this, however, the so-called "Free Syrian Army," according to the *New York Times*, consists of only 100 or so small formations made up of "a handful of fighters to a couple of hundred combatants," betraying the narrative that the Syrian government faces a large popular uprising, and revealing that the "Free Syrian Army" is in fact a small collection of mercenaries, foreign fighters, and sectarian extremists, armed, funded, and directed by foreign interests solely to wreak havoc within Syria. For the United States to claim Syria has "failed" to protect its population, while simultaneously fueling the very armed conflict it claims it is seeking to end, is not only hypocrisy of the highest order, but a crime against world peace - punishable under the Nuremberg precedent. Additionally, *TIME* Magazine's June 25, 2012 article "A War on Two Fronts," described how the US State Department budgeted over $72 million to train armed dissidents in encryption, hacking, and producing viral videos:

Washington has said it will not actively support the Syrian opposition in its bid to oust Assad. Officially, the U.S. says it abides by the U.N process led by Kofi Annan and does not condone arms sales to opposition groups as long as there are U.N. Observers in Syria. Nevertheless, as U.S. officials have revealed to TIME, the Obama Administration has been providing media-technology training and support to Syrian dissidents by way of small nonprofits like the Institute for War & Peace Reporting and Freedom House. Viral videos of alleged atrocities, like the footage Abu Ghassan produced, have made Assad one of the most reviled men on the planet, helping turn the Arab League against him and embarrassing his few remaining allies almost daily. "If the [U.S.] government is involved in Syria, the government isn't going to take direct responsibility for it," says Lawrence Lessig, director of Harvard's Edmond J. Safra Center for Ethics. "The tools that you deploy in Internet freedom interfere with tools deployed by an existing government, and that can be perceived as an act of aggression."

The program actually began four years ago with a different target: China. In 2008, Michael Horowitz, a longtime religious-liberty advocate, went to his friend Representative Frank Wolf, a Virginia Republican, and suggested setting aside funds to help Falun Gong, a religious group that Beijing has labeled a dangerous cult. The money was supposed to help the dissident distribute software to jump China's massive firewall and organize online as well as communicate freely with the outside world. Wolf succeeded in appropriating $15 million. But U.S. diplomats feared that move would derail relations with Beijing, and little money was spent. Then in 2009 – 10 Iranian protests and last year's Arab Spring made Internet freedom a much more fashionable term in Washington. Congress soon forked over an additional $57 million to State to spend in the next three years. The money is spilt among three areas: education and training; anonymization, which masks users' identities, usually through encryption; and circumvention technology, which allows users to overcome government censors so that their work – and that of repressive regimes – can be see worldwide.[96]

[96] Hillary's Little Startup: How the U.S. Is Using Technology to Aid Syria's Rebels, *TIME*, June 13, 2012

In brazen display of hypocrisy, the United States championed "Internet Freedom" against "repressive regimes" it sought to undermine and topple, while in 2012, US policy makers and representatives repeatedly authored and attempted to pass controversial internet censorship bills such as the Anti-Counterfeiting Trade Agreement (ACTA), which would have abolished all legal oversight involving the removal internet content, allowing copyright holders to force ISPs to remove material from the internet, something that would normally require a court order, thus mandating ISPs with legal liabilities if they chose not to remove content. Additionally under ACTA and similar regulatory proposals, internet users would be criminalized, barred from accessing the Internet and even imprisoned for sharing copyrighted material. US senators Joseph Lieberman and John McCain, both staunch supporters of foreign intervention in Syria, would issue S. 2105 (Cybersecurity Act) on February 15th, 2012 and S. 2151 (Secure IT) on March 1th, 2012. On April 26, 2012, the US House of Representatives passed the Cyber Intelligence Sharing and Protection Act (CISPA) – a law that would have starkly detrimental implications for the internet as a medium for free speech if signed into law by US President Barack Obama. While *TIME* reports that the US government's initial target was indeed China – with $15 million appropriated for cyber efforts to support dissident activity against Beijing – it was Joseph Lieberman himself who famously stated:

> *Right now China, the government, can disconnect parts of its Internet in case of war and we need to have that here too.*[97]

TIME's report reflects the seemingly limitless degree of outside interference in the Syrian conflict, with foreign entities attempting to meticulously cultivate and shape every dimension of the situation to the detriment of the legitimate government in Syria. *TIME* additionally reported that the Obama administration's executive order imposing sanctions on any company "helping Syria or Iran commit human-rights abuses" would not include the American companies that sold the Syrian government the internet technology it uses to filter its internet services, the very services the US government has allotted substantial public funds towards to train dissidents to bypass:

> *An ongoing challenge is that the flow of software goes to both sides. The regime has imported technology from the U.S. to track people online. "A lot of these technologies can be used for great good,' says Sascha Meinrath, who is leading the Internet-in-a-suitcase project, 'but they are also a Faustian bargain." The Obama Administration last month issued an Executive Order imposing sanctions on any company helping Syrian or Iran commit human-rights abuses. Washington's high-tech campaign will not dethrone Assad. But is has given Syrian dissidents a measure of confidence as they face the regime's advantage in firepower. In the months since finishing his training, Abu Ghassan has shot dozens of videos. Asked whether his AK-47 or his video camera is the more powerful weapon, Abu Ghassan laughs. "My AK!" he says. He pauses for a few seconds. "Actually if there is an Internet connection, my camera is more powerful."*

---

[97] Cybersecurity Measures Will Mandate Government "ID Tokens" To Use The Internet, Prison Planet, June 28, 2010

In late June 2012, a Turkish F-4 jet manufactured by the US and last used in major combat operations in Iraq to destroy air defenses, penetrated Syrian airspace and was shot down by Syrian security forces. Turkey would claim its jet was "a mile into international waters" by the time it was shot down. The F-4 fighter jet, the newest of which are already around 30 years old, has a top speed of Mach 2.2, or 1,600-mph / 2,500-kph. That means in one minute it can travel 26 miles - or nearly one mile every 2 seconds. Any anti-aircraft weapon fired against Turkey's admittedly "off course" fighter would have certainly been fired while the jet was well within Syrian airspace with the fired ordnance airborne and on course to intercepting the aircraft before it traveled back over international waters. Turkey's claim of being "a mile" within international airspace may seem reasonable to the average observer, accustomed to traveling at speeds where a mile is relatively far, but in terms of air combat, a mile equates into seconds. That means in one minute it can travel 26 miles - or nearly one mile every 2 seconds. Even if claims by Turkey are true that it had retreated to a "mile" over international waters when it was destroyed, that would mean it was over international waters for a mere 2 seconds. This means whatever ordnance Syria used was already fired and airborne in Syrian airspace before the aircraft departed.

Turkey, acutely aware of the immense tensions it has cultivated with neighboring Syria, exercised recklessness by traveling so close to Syrian airspace. The casual observer may also be unaware of the role US-built F-4's play in scouting out and neutralizing air defense systems. Designated "wild weasels," F-4's had been extensively used in the opening phases of war against Iraq in 1991, flying 2,596 sorties, firing more than 1,000 air-to-ground missiles, and destroying more than 200 targets in a campaign aimed at destroying Iraqi air defenses. Perhaps relying on the ignorance of their readership as to how speeds, trajectories, and weapons of modern warfare work, the mainstream press has attempted to portray the downing of the F-4 as a provocative act carried out entirely over international waters. In reality, Turkey's jet was fired upon in Syrian airspace, by its own account, as it was supposedly in "international space" for only one or two seconds before finally being struck. Syria claims the entire event took place over Syrian waters - a claim NATO has been unable to refute with anything more substantial than mere rhetoric.[98] Turkey would push NATO to regard Syria's actions as an attack on the alliance, prompting NATO to hold a meeting under Article 4 of the alliance's treaty, which allows a NATO member to request a consultation if it feels a threat to its territorial integrity or security. Turkey would vow "proportionate" retaliation for its downed jet, prompting Turkish Prime Minister Recep Erdoğan, to pledge "all possible support to liberate the Syrians from dictatorship" of Bashar al-Assad's government, offering support for Syrian rebels, warning that any Syrian troops approaching Turkish borders would be considered a threat and dealt with as a military target.

On June 27th, 2012, Turkey sent a heavily guarded convoy of 15 long-distance guns and other military vehicles to the Syrian border, amid belligerent threats of retaliation, prompting President Assad to acknowledge that his country was officially in a state of war, and that winning would depend on crushing the militant opposition. As the situation on the Turkish-Syrian border remained tense while

---

[98] Syria says it shot down Turkish jet over Syrian waters, NBC News, June 22, 2012

Turkish officials confirmed the deployment of 30 anti-aircraft batteries, the Turkish Defense Procurement Agency announced its plans to seek a $4 billion contract for a long-range air-defense missile system.[99] On June 28, 2012, two large bomb explosions targeting a government building rocked Damascus, prompting President Assad to reassert the Syrian government's duty to "annihilate terrorists in any corner of the country," adding:

We will not accept any non-Syrian, non-national model, whether it comes from big countries or friendly countries. No one knows how to solve Syria's problems as well as we do.

Kofi Annan proposed a new Syrian solution, mandating the creation of a transitional national unity government consisting of both representatives of Assad's government and members of the opposition to create a neutral backdrop for transition – insinuating that Assad would not have a place in the new government. Russia categorically opposed the idea that other countries should dictate the future of Syria, insisting that the decision be up to Syrians themselves. Russian Foreign Minister Sergey Lavrov stated:

We will not support and cannot support any meddling from outside or any imposition of recipes. This also concerns the fate of the president of the country, Bashar al-Assad.

The possibility of foreign military entities openly engaging in warfare against Syria remains ever present, with Turkey the likely candidate to lead the charge against Assad if the situation continues to deteriorate. With Turkey's ostensible need to annex regions of northern Syria to establish a series of long proposed "humanitarian corridors" as the pretext, a military intervention might be a possibility. Whether or not the Syrian crisis is met with open foreign military intervention, it is important to point out that, because of the covertly trained, armed and financed lawless rebel fighters, the Syrian people have already felt the horrors of war, in all its inane violence and unmitigated stupidity. While Kofi Annan's original Peace Plan – if honestly implemented with both sides respecting the ceasefire – would have defused the situation, it is Annan and the member nations of NATO and the Gulf Cooperation Council that disproportionately laid the blame for increasing violence solely on the Syrian government, while those nations took every measure possible to further enflame the situation by providing material assistance to sectarian extremists. Considering the level of subversion and deceit demonstrated by foreign powers operating in Syria, Bashar al-Assad's ambitions to crush sectarian fighters by force may well be warranted. As with many other Western-backed uprisings operating under the cover of "democratic" jargon, the use of violence, snipers, mercenaries, and other armed provocateurs is part of a long established pattern of national destabilization through the barrel of a gun. Undoubtedly, there will come a time when those responsible individuals answer for their crimes against the nation of Syria, and its people.

---

[99] Missile shopping: Turkey to buy long-range missile system, June 29, 2012

Chapter 2:
Perception Management and Psychological Warfare

"The business of the journalist is to destroy the truth, to lie outright, to pervert, to vilify, to fawn at the feet of mammon, and to sell the country for his daily bread. You know it and I know it, and what folly is this toasting an independent press. We are the tools and vassals of the rich men behind the scenes. We are the jumping jacks, they pull the strings and we dance. Our talents, our possibilities and our lives are all the property of other men. We are intellectual prostitutes."

John Swinton

Former Chief of Staff at The New York Times

Throughout the Syrian crisis, the portrayal of events on the ground by various news media outlets became an extension of the conflict itself – a battlefield of diametrically opposed views vying for legitimacy. Any reportage or analysis that diverted too far from the dominant narrative found no place in the Western mainstream media. State-sponsored English language news agencies such as *Russia Today*, Iran's *PressTV*, and numerous other outlets for independent research and analysis offered a different interpretation of events in Syria. To propagate their version of reality, reputable mainstream news outlets such as *BBC*, *CNN*, and *Al-Jazeera* were largely reliant on questionable *YouTube* video footage, social media hearsay and admittedly unconfirmed reports from members of the opposition. Numerous factual inconsistencies and official exaggerations followed, leading many to question the dominant narrative and the news outlets disseminating it.

While some authentic footage from inside Syria surfaced throughout the conflict, other videos featured members of the opposition "staging" acts of violence in settings that resembled movie-sets, complete with bandages and fake blood. Shortly after the start of the uprising, Israel's *Ynet News* published an article in late April 2011 citing claims by Syrian state media that security forces recovered bottles of blood, mobile phones using foreign SIM cards, positioning software and digital cameras containing fabricated videos depicting acts of violence.[1] *Ynet News* dismissed the claims as an act of desperation from Assad's regime to downplay violence, but offered no evidence beyond more "activist witness accounts". According to the report issued by Syria's *SANA News*, the phones and cameras were carried by members of an armed group responsible for attacking military personnel in the Rakhem al-Hirak area of Daraa:

Group members also carried clubs, swords and metal implements that were used during protests against security forces, in addition to bottles full of real blood to be used in filming fabricated acts of violence and bottles filled with gasoline to start fires.[2]

---

[1] Syria: Reports of violence fabricated, Ynet News, April 23, 2011
[2] Mobile Phones Using non-Syrian SIM Cards and Digital Cameras, SANA News, April 23, 2011

While Syrian state media reported numerous cases of rebel groups attacking military locations and staging acts of violence, the Western mainstream media cited ever-increasing casualty rates, relying on organizations based in the United Kingdom. Both the Syrian Observatory for Human Rights (SOHR) and the Syrian Human Rights Monitoring Centre (the latter having no web presence) compiled reports from "activists inside and outside the country," to produce the overwhelming casualty reports cited by mainstream media outlets. The United States government also financially supported Syrian Non-Governmental Organizations (NGOs) that provided the United Nations with its official casualty rates through organizations such as the National Endowment for Democracy and other institutions that receive funding directly from the US Congress and State Department.

Nearly every Syrian human rights organization whose findings have been acknowledged by the mainstream media interlock with seemingly benign NGOs and civil society groups that receive funding from corporations that actively interface with "global institutions," such as the International Monetary Fund, World Bank, the International Criminal Court, and the United Nations. *Reporters Without Borders* (a recipient of funds from the National Endowment for Democracy) released a March 2011 report titled, "Journalists targeted by governments desperate to control news," which cited the London-based Syrian Human Rights Monitoring Centre, while *Human Rights Watch* (a recipient of funds from George Soros' Open Society Institute) cited the Washington-based Damascus Center for Human Rights for its published reports.[3] Outlets such as the *Wall Street Journal* repeatedly mention Radwan Ziadeh, a Washington-based Syrian opposition activist and director of the Damascus Center for Human Rights Studies.[4] the *Boston Globe* in 2011 stated, "Activists said security forces killed at least 26 people and wounded hundreds," continuing, "Wissam Tarif, executive director of Insan, a Syrian human rights group, said he had interviewed young men tortured just days ago. One of them, who had his fingernails pulled out, had taken a lead in the protests yesterday in Baniyas."

While the authenticity of these reports remains difficult to confirm, the *Boston Globe*'s story can be perceived as misleading, as Wissam Tarif and his Insan organization were not on the ground bearing witness to events in Baniyas, but based in Spain, operating as an "international non-governmental organization." The *Guardian* noted the difficulties of verifying reports in an April 2011 article, quoting a *Human Rights Watch* researcher monitoring Syria from Beirut, Lebanon who said:

We are receiving second hand information from Deraa that is quite worrying about bodies on the ground, more than 30 people killed over the last two days, campaigns of arrests, but we are not able to confirm that.[5]

While it would be unwise to dismiss all allegations of excessive violence credited to Syrian security forces, there are firm grounds for skepticism with regard to reports of government-orchestrated massacres. Not only have such claims been fabricated in Syria, but also throughout the conflict in Libya in 2011. Unverified

---

[3] Journalists Targeted By Governments Desperate To Control The News, Reporters Without Borders, March 23, 2011
[4] Syria: Armed Opposition Groups Committing Abuses, Human Rights Watch, March 20, 2012
[5] Syria, Libya and Middle East unrest - Thursday 28 April 2011, The Guardian, April 28, 2011

reports accusing Muammar Gaddafi of strafing peaceful demonstrators with fighter jets and killing more than 6,000 civilians were the basis for the Libyan Jamahiriya government's expulsion from the UN Human Rights Council shortly before the UN Security Council issued Resolution 1973, which

One of the main sources for these allegations was the Libyan League for Human Rights, an organization linked to the International Federation of Human Rights, the FIDH (a recipient of funds from the US State Department). On February 21st, 2011, the General Secretary of the Libyan League for Human Rights, Dr. Soliman Bouchuiguir, initiated a petition in collaboration with UN Watch and the National Endowment for Democracy, which was later signed by over 70 NGOs. On the 25th of February 2011, Dr. Soliman Bouchuiguir went to the UN Human Rights council in Geneva to accuse the Libyan Jamahiriya government of committing crimes against humanity and hiring over 6,000 mercenaries to "pillage and kill all civilians without distinction." French investigative journalist Julien Teil's 2011 documentary film, "*The Humanitarian War*," reveals the tenuous fabrications of these allegations in an interview with Dr. Soliman Bouchuiguir:

Julien Teil: *You describe a lot of crime in Libya, for example on March 17th, you reported six thousand dead, twelve thousand wounded, five hundred missing, seven hundred cases of rape, and seventy five thousand refugees. On May 31st, you reported eighteen thousand dead, forty six thousand wounded, twenty eight thousand missing, one thousand six hundred cases of rape, and one hundred and fifty thousand refugees. If we go to Libya, what would you advise us to do in order to document all those crimes?*

Dr. Soliman Bouchuiguir: *There is no way. You know, the Libyan government never gives information on human rights, on prisons, prisoners, and people who have been killed, on people being killed... so an estimation has to be done. And I did not get this information from just anyone. I got that from the Libyan Prime Minister, on the other side, so of the National Transitional Council. It's the Prime Minister, Mister... uhhh... wait... I'll tell you later... It was Mahmoud of the Warfallah tribe! He's the one that stated and gave these numbers. I used them, but with some precaution.*

At a press conference on June 28th, 2011, International Criminal Court prosecutor Luis Moreno Ocampo responded to a question regarding the evidence used by the ICC to issue an arrest warrant for Muammar Gaddafi, Saif Al Islam, and Abdullah Al Senussi. He stated:

I advise you to read the application of the prosecutor's office, many pages, I think what... 77 pages. We describe in detail the facts, most of it is public, and the judges also decided and analyzed the evidence, so of course, we are prosecutors and judges, so rely on facts. So, we proved the crimes, that's what we did, we presented the case to judges, and for a month and ten days, the judges from three different continents made an independent evaluation and they decided.

Most of the document referred to by Ocampo was heavily redacted, withholding crucial pieces of evidence from public scrutiny. Pages 17 to 71 were redacted, precisely the sections disclosing evidence and testimony of alleged atrocities committed by the Libyan Jamahiriya government. Amongst the public sources cited by the prosecutor's office at the ICC, were *FOX News* articles, documents released by the Central Intelligence Agency, and press releases issued by Dr. Soliman Bouchuiguir's Libyan League for Human Rights, including a speech he gave at the UN Human Rights Council citing allegations given to him by the NTC's then-Prime Minister Mahmoud Jabril.

Julien Teil: The Human Rights Council, where you gave your speech, did not investigate the information you provided before the UN Security Council used them. How do you explain the lack of investigation and testimony that led directly to a United Nations Resolution? Why is it that your speech had such an impact and that the NGO consortium you gathered succeeded in seizing the Human Rights Council so the Security Council got involved and decided a resolution?

Dr. Soliman Bouchuiguir: I think the decisive fact is that Gaddafi used the air force against his own people, and I think that opened the way for... the use of the air force against his own people showed that he was unstoppable. In Benghazi, more than three hundred people died in two days – in two days! More than three hundred victims! And that was all on paper, even the names.

Julien Teil: Yes, but about the six thousand dead, twelve thousand wounded, five hundred missing, seven hundred cases of rape and seventy five thousand refugees, can you give us any evidence?

Dr. Soliman Bouchuiguir: Now there are one hundred and fifty thousand refugees in Tunisia only. Go ask the Tunisian government, it's the Tunisian government that stated that! Now there are more than one hundred and fifty thousand Libyans in Tunisia who filed refugee claims in Tunisia.

Julien Teil: About the number of people killed, can you give us any evidence?

Dr. Soliman Bouchuiguir: ...What?

Julien Teil: About the number of people killed, can you give us any evidence?

Dr. Soliman Bouchuiguir: There is no evidence. What I can tell you is that there is no... there are no documents - in Az-Zawiya, eighteen thousand people died, were injured or missing. Eighteen thousand people! In Az-Zawiya only! [6]

While *Al-Jazeera* and *BBC* reported that the Libyan Jamahiriya government inflicted airstrikes on Benghazi in an attempt to quell popular demonstrations, Russia's military released a report stating that Libya was being monitored from space and no such attacks actually took place, suggesting that these events were fabricated entirely.[7] Dr. Soliman Bouchuiguir's Libyan League for Human Rights and 70 other affiliated NGOs sent letters to President Obama, European Union High Representative Catherine Ashton, and the UN Secretary-General Ban-ki Moon, demanding international action against Libya by invoking the "Responsibility to Protect" doctrine, allowing NATO to militarily intervene in Libya. The evidence cited by Libyan League for Human Rights has never been verified, nor has it been made available for public scrutiny by the International Criminal Court – evidence that was

---

[6] The Humanitarian War, Julien Teil, 2011
[7] "Airstrikes in Libya did not take place" – Russian military, Russia Today, March 01, 2011

fabricated and used as the basis for the National Transition Council to seize control of Libya in collaboration with NATO.

Bouchuiguir conceded that these allegations were entirely reliant on the opposition National Transitional Council, particularly on the NTC's former Prime Minister Mahmoud Jabril. Jabril was CEO of the international firm *JTrack*, which offered personal training in communications skills to Arab and Southeast Asian political leaders backed by the United States and Israel. A primary client of Jabril's was Sheikh Hamad bin-Khalifa Al Thani, the ruling Emir of Qatar and principle financier of the *Al-Jazeera* news network. Qaradawi, host of the program *"ash-Shariah wal-Hayat" ("Shariah and Life")* on *Al-Jazeera's* Arabic language service is noted for enflaming divisions in the Islamic World by referring to Shi'as heretics, for demanding support for the Libyan rebels and for issuing a fatwa against Muammar Gaddafi, calling for his execution:

...To the officers and the soldiers who are able to kill Muammar Gaddafi, to whoever among them is able to shoot him with a bullet and to free the country and [God's] servants from him, I issue this fatwa (uftî): Do it! [8] [9]

It was during the "Arab Spring" uprisings that Wadah Khanfar dramatically shifted *Al-Jazeera's* editorial policy in a move that French journalist Thierry Meyssan called a complete loss of the channels credibility, something that "took 15 years to build and only 6 months to lose." In his September 2011 article, "Wadah Khanfar, Al-Jazeera and the triumph of televised propaganda," Meyssan stated:

During the first half of 2011, the Qatari channel became the preferred instrument for pro-Western propaganda: it went to great lengths to obscure the anti-imperialist and anti-Zionist aspect of the Arab revolutions and, in each country, it picked the actors it intended to support and those it decided to deprecate. Not surprisingly, it supported the king of Bahrain, a student of Mahmoud Jibril, who had his people gunned down, while Al-Jazeera's spiritual counsellor, Sheikh al-Qaradawi, was calling for a Jihad over the air against al-Gaddafi and al-Assad, falsely accusing them of murdering their own people.

The conversion of Al-Jazeera into a propaganda tool for the recolonisation of Libya was not achieved without the knowledge of the emir of Qatar, but indeed under his leadership. The Gulf Cooperation Council was the first to call for an armed intervention in Libya; Qatar was the first Arab country to join the Contact Group. He funneled weapons to the Libyan "rebels" before sending in his own ground troops, especially during the Battle of Tripoli. In exchange, he obtained the privilege of controlling all the oil trade on behalf of the National Transitional Council. [10]

With Mahmoud Jabril at the helm of the officially recognized rebel government of Libya, replicas were built of Tripoli's Green Square and Bab-el-Azizia in Al-Jazeera's studios in Doha, where fabricated footage was broadcasted depicting rebels capturing Tripoli, a full three days before the event actually occurred amid heavy bombardments from NATO in support of the armed rebels. Although Libyan state

---

[8] The Politics of Sects, Al-Ahram, September 25, 2008
[9] The fatwa of Shaykh Yûsuf al-Qaradâwî against Gaddafi, Hartford Seminary, March 15, 2011
[10] Wadah Khanfar, Al-Jazeera and the triumph of televised propaganda, September 26, 2011

media issued reports warning of video fabrication several days before the act was carried out, the plan was implemented nonetheless. This elaborate psychological warfare operation was intended to diminish loyalty and public confidence in Tripoli and throughout the country. Throughout the conflict in Libya, the armed forces of the Libyan Jamahiriya government were referred to as pro-Gaddafi mercenaries. These accusations, repeated by multiple news agencies, were based on the assertion, repeated ad nauseum, that Gaddafi hired several thousand African mercenaries who were reportedly killing civilians and using rape as a weapon. On February 22nd, 2011, *France24* interviewed the President of *Amnesty International France*, Genevieve Garrigos, where she claimed that Libyan Jamahiriya government employed the use of foreign fighters, stating:

On Friday and Saturday, we received information that foreign mercenaries could be fighting among the Gaddafi forces sent against those protestors in order to accelerate the process of oppression.

Five months after her appearance on France24, Julien Teil interviewed Garrigos, only to find that her position had completely changed on the matter:

Julien Teil: *Amnesty International's advisor Donatella Rovera was in Libya for three months. She observed the imprisonment of captured Libyan civilians and foreigners by the National Transitional Council, who presented these detainees as foreign mercenaries. What can you tell us about that?*

Genevieve Garrigos: *Since the beginning of the deployment of anti-Gaddafi troops, there were rumors of mercenary forces acting on behalf of Gaddafi, yet our investigators who arrived in mid-February and departed in late June established that only a small number of people were incarcerated without charges. Actually, those rumors mostly accused dark colored people or black people – they could have been Libyans, since Libyans living in the South of the country don't necessarily have Arab features. This created a kind of fear and xenophobia, which led to beating, mistreatment and a few imprisonments. But today, we have to admit that we have no evidence Gaddafi employed mercenary forces.*

Julien Teil: *Your colleague reported that she didn't witness any mercenaries, and that this was an unverified story spread by the media. Can you confirm her assertions?*

Genevieve Garrigos: *Absolutely! Donatella's work – and this is why we sent investigators in early – was to verify if we actually found mercenaries, and we didn't. For instance, she quotes a young Algerian, whose boss had to testify he worked in a bakery because he was suspected to be a mercenary. Currently, we have no sign or evidence to corroborate these rumors.*[11]

The circulation of false reports of Muammar Gaddafi employing African mercenary fighters indeed enflamed feelings of xenophobia among Libya's rebels, leading to the widespread persecution, detainment, and murder of dark-skinned Libyans, as well as migrant workers from Niger and Chad.[12] The propagation of such unsubstantiated claims provided the necessary pretext for foreign intervention in

---

[11] The Humanitarian War, Julien Teil, 2011
[12] Libya: Stop Arbitrary Arrests of Black Africans, Human Rights Watch, September 4, 2011

Libya. This military and media campaign was achieved through the collaboration of institutions such as the UN and ICC, in partnership with corporate-owned news media outlets and a myriad of civil society groups, most of which receive financial assistance from the US State Department. It is through these distorted lenses that the Syrian conflict must be interpreted.

Wall Street and London's media machine eagerly churned out headlines like *BBC*'s November 2011 article, "Syria security forces 'commit crimes against humanity,'" announcing the conclusions of a UN Human Rights Council report regarding the ongoing violence in Syria.[13] Despite the fact that personnel and journalists from over 200 international media institutions have been allowed to enter Syria legally since the outbreak of the crisis, the *BBC* article claims, "the investigation team members say they were denied entry into Syria itself," and that the entirety of their "evidence" was garnered solely from interviews with "223 victims, witnesses and also army defectors to investigate alleged human rights violations." *BBC*'s article raises immediate suspicion over the veracity of the report, as "victims, witnesses, and defectors," interviewed outside of Syria constitutes more hearsay than evidence, by groups of people with a vested interest in negatively portraying the Syrian government. The November 2011 UN Human Rights Council report on Syria describes exactly "how" the text was compiled. The section titled "Methods of Work," describes the questionable means of aggregating evidence for the report, demonstrating an immense conflict of interest behind the UN's predetermined conclusion – that Syria is guilty of "crimes against humanity" and that the UN Security Council must act (emphasis added):

C. Methods of work

*7. First-hand information was collected through interviews with victims and witnesses of events in the Syrian Arab Republic. **The interviewing process began in Geneva** on 26 September 2011. Overall, 223 victims and/or witnesses, including personnel who defected from the military and the security forces, were interviewed.*

*8. **A public call was made to all interested persons and organizations to submit relevant information and documentation** that would help the commission implement its mandate. It held meetings with Member States from all regional groups, regional organizations, including the League of Arab States and the Organization of Islamic Cooperation, **non- governmental organizations, human rights defenders, journalists and experts**. Reports, scholarly analyses and media accounts, as well as audio and visual material, were also duly considered.*

*9. **The information collected is stored in a secure database governed by United Nations rules on confidentiality.***

10. The protection of victims and witnesses lies at the heart of the methodology of human rights investigations. While the collected information remains confidential, the commission is deeply concerned about the possibility of reprisals against individuals who cooperated with it, and against their relatives in the Syrian Arab Republic. It is

---

[13] Syria security forces 'commit crimes against humanity,' BBC, November 28, 2011

also concerned about the protection of those individuals who openly spoke to the media
in an attempt to counter the news blockade imposed by the Government.[14]

The UNHRC report would also state that it received no cooperation from the Syrian government, ostensibly verifying grievances that the publication is but a one-sided exercise to provide the worst possible image of the Syrian government, as told by the Syrian opposition. The inclusion of non-governmental organizations raises immediate concerns, especially considering that the report is entirely negligent in listing any of these contributing NGOs, who are more than likely espousing the dominant narrative championed by the National Endowment for Democracy, George Soros' Open Society Institute, and their numerous of subsidiaries. The term "alleged" is used throughout the report in various forms, further illustrating the tenuous nature of the UN Human Rights Council's "evidence," while all of the testimony, those who supplied it, and apparently the NGOs involved in compiling the UN report are expectedly kept "confidential." The US National Endowment for Democracy's journal, *Democracy Digest*, in their August 2011 article titled, "Syrian military 'strained', as Clinton meets opposition activists," noted several NGOs reporting human rights abuses in Syria, citing the London-based Syrian Observatory for Human Rights, along with the Washington-based Damascus Center for Human Rights.[15]

Syrian Observatory for Human Rights head, Rami Abdelrahman, met directly with British Foreign Minister William Hague, who similarly coddled Libyan opposition leaders in London while playing a key role in promoting the NATO attack on Libya. Just as in Libya, where "human rights activists" have now admitted to fabricating evidence used by the International Criminal Court and the United Nations, the "evidence" from Syria remains "confidential," and thus, impossible to confirm. The Syrian Observatory for Human Rights serves as one of the exclusive sources of evidence of human rights violations in Syria, although the Observatory itself fails to publish its financial statements or the backgrounds of those that constitute its membership. Throughout the crisis in Syria, news agencies such as *AFP, AP, CNN, MSNBC, CBS, BBC,* and many of the largest Western newspapers cited the Observatory, creating an impression of a sprawling organization with hundreds of members working on the ground, documenting evidence in Syria with photographs and video, while coordinating with foreign press to transparently and objectively "observe" the "human rights" conditions in Syria, as well as demonstrate their methodologies. A December 2011 *Reuters* piece titled, "Coventry - an unlikely home to prominent Syria activist" provides further insight in the Observatory and its operator, Rami Abdelrahman:

With only a few hours sleep, a phone glued to his ear and another two ringing, the fast-talking director of arguably Syria's most high-profile human rights group is a very busy man. "Are there clashes? How did he die? Ah, he was shot," said Rami Abdulrahman into a phone, the talk of gunfire and death incongruous with his two bedroom terraced home in Coventry, from where he runs the Syrian Observatory for Human Rights. When he isn't fielding calls from international media, Abdulrahman is a few minutes down the road at his clothes shop, which he runs with his wife. Cited by

---

[14] UN Human Rights Council Report on Syria, United Nations, November 2011
[15] Syrian military 'strained', as Clinton meets opposition activists, Democracy Digest, August 02, 2011

virtually every major news outlet since an uprising against the iron rule of Syrian President Bashar al-Assad began in March, the observatory has been a key source of news on the events in Syria. Surrounded by the trappings of family life – a glitter-spangled card made by his young daughter, a monkey doll with "Best Dad" on its belly – Abdulrahman sits with a laptop and phones and pieces together accounts of conflict and rights abuses before uploading news to the internet.[16]

Abdulrahman admits that he fled Syria over 10 years ago and has lived in Britain ever since, and will not return until "al-Assad goes." The opportunity for impropriety seems almost inevitable for a man who openly berates a government long targeted for "regime change" by the very country he currently resides in, and whose method of reportage involves dubious phone-calls, which remain difficult for anyone to verify. When Abdulrahman isn't receiving phone calls from fellow opposition members in Syria or passing on his less-than-reputable information to the Western press, he has been seen slinking in and out of the British Foreign Office to meet directly with Foreign Secretary William Hague - who also openly seeks the removal of Syrian President, Bashar al-Assad. Given the lack of credibility and the obvious disadvantage of being nearly 3,000 miles away from the alleged subject of his "observations," Abdulrahman is a compromised source of information for any outside observer seeking credible information on the conflict in Syria, one who has every reason to twist reality to suit his admittedly politically-motivated agenda of toppling the government in Damascus.

Throughout the conflict in Syria, outlets such as *BBC* and *CNN* embraced English speaking opposition activists on the ground in Syria, most prominently British-Syrian dual national Danny Dayem or "Syrian Danny." Dayem claimed to have aspirations to join the Free Syrian Army, and often called for the implementation of a no fly zone, pleading for the United States, Israel, and NATO to conduct airstrikes against Syrian air bases.[17] Dayem's credibility plummeted when footage leaked of him staging sounds of gunfire and exhibiting relaxed behavior off camera, before going into character for a hysterical "casualty report" during an interview with Anderson Cooper of *CNN*. Cooper attempted to vindicate Dayem on his program, insisting that networks like *CNN* were forced to rely on activist media that "cannot be independently confirmed," despite the fact that Dayem displayed great difficulty verbally attempting to exonerate himself after leaked footage showed him asking, "Did you tell him to get the gunfire ready?" On air, Dayem nervously stated, "I don't know how they got it, this is all private, we should have, this has all been deleted, we have to delete all this stuff," while Cooper completely failed to address what was essentially an open admission of fabrication.

Amina Abdallah Arraf al Omari, a lesbian Syrian activist calling for increased political and personal freedoms, was at one point a prominent English language blogger. Omari's popular blog, "A Gay Girl In Damascus," received attention from mainstream media outlets such as the *Guardian*, who affirmed that the blog was "increasingly popular after capturing the imagination of the Syrian opposition as the protest movement struggled in the face of the government crackdown." In a May

---

[16] Coventry - an unlikely home to prominent Syria activist, Reuters, August 12, 2011
[17] Syria: Life Under Fire, CNN, February 12, 2012

2011 article titled, "A Gay Girl in Damascus becomes a heroine of the Syrian revolt," the *Guardian* wrote:

She is perhaps an unlikely hero of revolt in a conservative country. Female, gay and half-American, Amina Abdullah is capturing the imagination of the Syrian opposition with a blog that has shot to prominence as the protest movement struggles in the face of a brutal government crackdown. Her blog really took off two weeks ago with a post entitled My Father the Hero, a moving account of how her father faced down two security agents who came to arrest her, accusing her of being a Salafist and a foreign agent.

Abdullah's family is well-connected – she has relatives in the government and the Muslim Brotherhood whom she prefers not to name – and she says being politically active was a "natural thing". "Unfortunately, for most of my life being aware of Syrian politics means simply observing and only commenting privately." That changed when protests broke out and Abdullah joined them, blogging about her experiences. "Teargas was lobbed at us. I saw people vomiting from the gas as I covered my own mouth and nose and my eyes burned," she wrote after one demonstration. "I am sure I wasn't the only one to note that, if this becomes standard practice, a niqab is a very practical thing to wear in future." [18]

Syrian security forces abducted Omari in 2011 during the uprising, prompting an international outcry from LGBT communities and the international media. 'A Gay Girl in Damascus' Blogger Kidnapped at Gunpoint in Syria, accusing Syrian state security services and Ba'ath Party militia of the abduction, while the US State Department showed concern.[19] Amid a campaign of international condemnation of Omari's aduction, a 40 year-old American writer Tom MacMaster admitted that the "inspiring hero of the Syrian revolution" was in fact an elaborate fictional character he concocted.

While entirely fictional claims of "Amina Arraf al Omari" being abducted by Syrian security forces were given credibility by the Western media, similar hysterics were cast over reports of 18-year-old, Zainab al-Hosni who was allegedly found beheaded and mutilated "apparently by Syrian security agents," while in custody after being "detained by security agents to pressure her activist brother to turn himself in," as cited in a dramatic report in the *Huffington Post*.[20] The report made every attempt to emphasize the Syrian's government's role in her killing, stating, "the Assad family has kept an iron grip on power in Syria for more than 40 years by brutally crushing every sign of dissent." However, days later, Zainab al-Hosni resurfaced, alive and well, on a Syrian State TV broadcast. The *Huffington Post*'s follow-up, "Zainab Al-Hosni, Woman Reported Beheaded, Allegedly Appears On TV," states:

A woman appeared on Syrian state television Wednesday claiming that she is the young Syrian who was widely reported to have been beheaded and mutilated by security agents while in custody last month. The station said the interview was intended to discredit foreign "media fabrications." In the state television interview, a

---

[18] A Gay Girl in Damascus becomes a heroine of the Syrian revolt, The Guardian, May 6, 2011

[19] 'A Gay Girl in Damascus' Blogger Kidnapped at Gunpoint in Syria, FOX News, June 07, 2011

[20] Syria: Zainab Al Hosni Believed To Be Killed In Custody, September 23, 2011

black-clad young woman who identified herself as Zainab al-Hosni said she had run away from her family home in late July because her brothers allegedly abused her. She said her family did not know that she was alive and she asked her mother for forgiveness. "I am very much alive and I have opted to tell the truth because I am planning to get married in the future and have kids who I want to be registered," she said. [21]

Media outlets irresponsibly distorted legitimate concerns regarding homosexuals and women in conflict-torn areas of Syria in an attempt to baselessly demonize the Assad government in step with the US State Department and its vast stable of media and intelligence assets. In the context of the 2011 Libyan uprising, Western media outlets hysterically reported that Muammar Gaddafi personally ordered the raping of hundreds of women, an unverified claim that senior US officials such as Ambassador Susan Rice asserted to leverage in support of UN Resolution 1973:

The reported crimes and human rights violations of the Gaddafi regime are awful enough as they are that one has to wonder why anyone would need to invent stories, such as that of Gaddafi's troops, with erections powered by Viagra, going on a rape spree. Perhaps it was peddled because it's the kind of story that "captures the imagination of traumatized publics". This story was taken so seriously that some people started writing to Pfizer to get it to stop selling Viagra to Libya, since its product was allegedly being used as a weapon of war. People who otherwise should know better, set out to deliberately misinform the international public.

The Viagra story was first disseminated by Al Jazeera, in collaboration with its rebel partners, favoured by the Qatari regime that funds Al Jazeera. It was then redistributed by almost all other major Western news media. Luis Moreno-Ocampo, Chief Prosecutor of the International Criminal Court, appeared before the world media to say that there was "evidence" that Gaddafi distributed Viagra to his troops in order "to enhance the possibility to rape" and that Gaddafi ordered the rape of hundreds of women. Moreno-Ocampo insisted: "We are getting information that Gaddafi himself decided to rape" and that "we have information that there was a policy to rape in Libya those who were against the government". He also exclaimed that Viagra is "like a machete," and that "Viagra is a tool of massive rape".

In a startling declaration to the UN Security Council, U.S. Ambassador Susan Rice also asserted that Gaddafi was supplying his troops with Viagra to encourage mass rape. She offered no evidence whatsoever to back up her claim. Indeed, U.S. military and intelligence sources flatly contradicted Rice, telling NBC News that "there is no evidence that Libyan military forces are being given Viagra and engaging in systematic rape against women in rebel areas." By June 10, Cherif Bassiouni, who is leading a UN rights inquiry into the situation in Libya, suggested that the Viagra and mass rape claim was part of a "massive hysteria". In fact, Bassiouni's team "uncovered only four alleged cases" of rape and sexual abuse: "Can we draw a conclusion that there is a systematic policy of rape? In my opinion we can't".

In addition to the UN, Amnesty International's Donatella Rovera said in an interview with the French daily Libération, that Amnesty had "not found cases of

---

rape.... Not only have we not met any victims, but we have not even met any persons who have met victims. As for the boxes of Viagra that Gaddafi is supposed to have had distributed, they were found intact near tanks that were completely burnt out." [22]

The organization *Women Under Siege* accused Syrian security forces of indiscriminately raping young women and committing other heinous acts in their publication, "The ultimate assault: Charting Syria's use of rape to terrorize its people." *Women Under Siege* reports of multiple attackers, "usually government forces", who are said to gang rape women in their homes, allegedly inoculating the victims to immobilize them while their "genitals are burned or filled with mice". Unquestionably, these acts warrant severe condemnation, however its relationship with reality remains unclear, as the report familiarly goes on to state (emphasis added):

***Government forces and others** appear to be carrying out appalling sexualized attacks against women, men, and children in Syria as the conflict there continues. **Although we are unable to independently confirm these stories**—Syria is simply too dangerous, and our research staff too small—they are **consistent both internally and within the news and NGO reports telling similar stories** from the Syrian conflict.*

Given the duplicity of the mainstream news media and associated NGOs in their coverage of the Syrian conflict, the credibility of any organization attempting to legitimize alleged reports of atrocities by citing their consistency to fit within a flawed dominant narrative remains highly questionable, especially when the organization itself concedes:

There are well-documented challenges and limitations when it comes to studying sexualized violence in conflict, and our data is not meant to represent the Syrian conflict in its entirety. All of our reports come second-or third-hand, and can't be independently confirmed.

Given these statements, the statistics of rape and violence issued by *Women Under Siege* can be nothing but highly questionable and marred with inconsistencies, culminating in what is essentially manipulative propaganda reliant on leveraging human rights abuses, while actively supporting a interventionist status quo from which numerous documented abuses have originated. While the organization acknowledges that its reports are unverified, statistics like the one below display the clear politicization of their purpose:

Government perpetrators have committed the majority of the attacks we've been able to track: 61 percent, including attacks against men and women, with another 6 percent carried out by government and shabiha forces together. These soldiers or officers have allegedly carried out 58 percent of rapes against women; shabiha (plainclothes militia) attackers 14 percent; government and shabiha working together 5 percent; and another or unknown attacker 26 percent. In 42 percent of the incidents of sexualized violence against women that we found, the victims were allegedly

---

[22] The Top Ten Myths in the War Against Libya, Counterpunch, August 31, 2012

attacked by multiple people at once, suggesting a disturbingly high rate of gang rape.
[23]

Further insight into the Women Under Siege organization can be gained from examining the background of the group's founder, feminist leader Gloria Steinem. An article published on February 21, 1967 in the *New York Times* titled, "C.I.A. Subsidized Festival Trips: Hundreds of Students Were Sent to World Gatherings," reports that Steinem was recruited by the CIA in 1958 to direct an activist organization called the "Independent Research Service," intended to promote left-liberalism in opposition to Marxism.[24] While receiving backing from the CIA, Steinem attended Communist-sponsored youth festivals throughout Europe, distributed newspapers, reported on other participants, and helped to incite riots. Women Under Siege is a project of Steinem's "Women's Media Center," which is itself a spinoff of its umbrella organization, Ms. Foundation, which receives direct funding from George Soros' Open Society Institute, the Ford Foundation, Tides Foundation, New York Life, Google, the United Nations, AT&T, Lifetime, the ACLU, and others as stated in their 2011 Annual Report.[25] Undoubtedly, Steinem's organization is co-facilitating the agenda of the US State Department, the National Endowment for Democracy, and the various intelligence and military agencies involved in destabilizing Syria and toppling its government.

The duplicitous editorial policies of Western mainstream media institutions and affiliated NGOs have worked to project a version of reality entirely friendly to American foreign policy objectives, including the condemnation of countries that stood against international resolutions mandating intervention in Syria. *Amnesty International's* campaign, "Russia: No More Excuses, Stand Up Against Bloodshed in Syria," encouraged readers to send pre-written messages to Russian Foreign Minister Sergei Lavrov and Ambassador Sergey Kislyak, urging them to halt arms shipments to the Syrian government and endorse an International Criminal Court indictment against Bashar al-Assad:

I appeal to you to ensure that the Security Council refers Syria to the International Criminal Court for crimes against humanity and other violations of international law; freezes the assets of President Bashar al-Assad and his close associates; and imposes an immediate arms embargo on Syria. [26]

While the idea of an arms embargo against Syria may initially sound plausible, the conduct of intelligence agencies such as the CIA and other supporters of Syria's armed insurgents unwaveringly confirms that such an embargo would be marginally implemented and completely disregarded with respect to arming insurgents. *Amnesty International* perversely attempts to twist around violence and unrest clearly fomented by the covert Western and Gulf presence inside Syria as somehow the result of Russia's refusal to capitulate in the face of another NATO intervention.

---

[23] The ultimate assault: Charting Syria's use of rape to terrorize its people, Women Under Siege, July 11, 2012

[24] C.I.A. Subsidized Festival Trips: Hundreds of Students Were Sent to World Gatherings, The New York Times, February 21, 1967

[25] 2011 Annual Report, Ms. Foundation, 2012

[26] Russia: No More Excuses, Stand Up Against Bloodshed in Syria, Amnesty International, 2012

Amnesty's report cites the fabricated death toll produced by the UN based solely on Syrian opposition claims, before bemoaning the positioning of Syrian troops and equipment in and around the city of Homs, which was known to be a prominent base of operations for heavily armed militants working against Syrian security forces. As organizations like *Amnesty International* (recipients of funding directly from the US State Department) naively address their readership with statements like, "Donate Now: Fight bad guys with every dollar," posing rhetorical questions such as, "How many more victims must suffer before Russia takes a decisive stance against crimes against humanity in Syria?" it becomes apparent that *Amnesty International* is working in contradiction of their own mission statement to "protect people wherever justice, freedom, truth and dignity are denied."

Suzanne Nossel, Executive Director of *Amnesty International*, had just finished a stint as Deputy Assistant Secretary for International Organizations at the US State Department before being appointed as head of *Amnesty*; she was also vice-president of strategy and operations for the *Wall Street Journal,* and a media and entertainment consultant at McKinsey & Company (a Council on Foreign Relations "founding" corporate member).[27] Upon closer examination of *Amnesty International* and similar organizations, it remains bewildering that such institutions can be considered impartial, when those who clearly represent American foreign policy interests constitute the groups' administration. Furthermore, *Amnesty International* receives funding from George Soros' Open Society Institute, as well as the UK Department for International Development, the European Commission and other corporate-funded foundations.[28] These staggering conflicts of interest arise from organizations, funded and run by representatives of Western governments and corporations, which disingenuously leverage noble causes, such as the preeminence of human rights, to carry out a self-serving political agenda.

On May 28, 2012, the *BBC* would admit to using a photograph taken of a 2003 massacre in Iraq for their depiction of the massacre in Houla, Syria, prompting the photographer who took the original photo, Marco di Lauro, to state, "someone is using someone else's picture for propaganda on purpose." An article published by the *Telegraph* in response to the situation stated:

Photographer Marco di Lauro said he nearly "fell off his chair" when he saw the image being used, and said he was "astonished" at the failure of the corporation to check their sources. The picture, which was actually taken on March 27, 2003, shows a young Iraqi child jumping over dozens of white body bags containing skeletons found in a desert south of Baghdad. It was posted on the BBC news website today under the heading "Syria massacre in Houla condemned as outrage grows". The caption states the photograph was provided by an activist and cannot be independently verified, but says it is "believed to show the bodies of children in Houla awaiting burial." [29]

This incident further encourages skepticism of unverified "evidence" brought forth by "pro-democracy activists," once again challenging the veracity of the dominant narrative shaping the Syrian crisis. Following the international hysteria

---

27 Hillary Clinton aide at the helm of Amnesty International USA, VoltaireNet, November 23, 2011
28 Report and financial statements for the year ended 31 March 2011, Amnesty International, 2011
29 BBC News uses 'Iraq photo to illustrate Syrian massacre,' The Telegraph, May 27, 2012

created by the Houla massacre, outlets such as the *Guardian* accused the Syrian military of "shelling" victims in their homes as reported in an article titled, "Syria shelling 'kills at least 90,'" containing a statement by UK Foreign Office Minister Alistair Burt claiming the deaths were the result of artillery.[30] Following a report from the Russian Foreign Ministry presenting evidence that members of the opposition took part in the massacre by employing the use of short-range weaponry, the *Guardian* shifted its narrative in the article, "Houla massacre survivor tells how his family were slaughtered," familiarly citing anonymous accounts of villagers crediting members of pro-government paramilitaries with the slaughter.[31] [32] The emotionally manipulative narrative comes straight from a nameless boy allegedly produced by "a town elder who is a member of the Syrian Revolutionary Council," before stating "We are unable to independently verify the account and have chosen not to name the boy for security reasons."

While the testimony put forth by this witness is undeniably harrowing, the *Guardian*'s revised account specifically cites the nameless boy supplied by the opposition, who claims to have seen Syrian troops dismount from their tanks and kill his entire family in front of him. Paradoxically, the *Guardian* then claims they weren't troops, but rather "al-Shabiha" irregular forces that dismounted from armored vehicles with "guns and knives." Answering a question as to how the witness knew the gunmen were pro-regime militiamen, he responded, "Why are you asking me who they were? I know who they were. We all know it. They were the regime army and people who fight with them. That is true." The *Guardian*'s report failed to corroborate or verify any of the claims presented by the anonymous young witness. Similarly, the *Guardian* claims in the article, "I saw massacre of children, says defecting Syrian air force officer," that long-bearded men with shaved heads were observed by an alleged "Air Force officer" from inside his house some 300 meters away, storming the village of Houla, Syria screaming, "Shabiha forever, for your eyes, Assad." The *Guardian* claims this tenuous narrative constitutes "crucial evidence on the Houla killings."

The officer claims he saw militants riding in "cars and army trucks and on motorbikes," which contradicts the testimony of the previous witness the *Guardian* has produced, who maintains that militants dismounted from tanks and armored transports to carry out the killings. "'They came in armored vehicles and there were some tanks,' said the boy." This discrepancy is never explained, and the *Guardian* is unable to confirm the identity of the bearded men, the officer's identity and his story. Additionally, the *Guardian* fails to explain how, from 300 meters inside his home, the "officer" was able to discern the identity of the men, what they were doing, or hear what they were saying. 300 meters (approximately the length of three football fields) is beyond the range of both a human's ability to discern what a human voice is saying, as well as beyond the ability for human eyes to positively identify strangers as belonging to one group of militants or another. According to *Guardian*'s "defected officer," he was able to discern the unfolding events from such a distance, with

---

[30] Syria shelling 'kills at least 90, The Guardian, May 26, 2012
[31] Both parties guilty in Houla massacre – Lavrov, Russia Today, May 28, 2012
[32] Houla massacre survivor tells how his family were slaughtered, The Guardian, May 28, 2012

artillery and assault rifles firing, no less. Throughout the crisis in Syria, both the *Guardian* and the *BBC* have demonstratively failed to provide any actual evidence to back the narrative they have been irresponsibly reported in Houla.[33]

A disturbing and very telling incident that unfolded in early June 2012 saw British *Channel 4's* Alex Thomson - one of the few Western journalists not only in Syria legally, but attempting to cover both sides of the conflict - purposefully led by rebels into a trap designed to have him and his team killed by government troops in order to use his death as propaganda. "Set up to be shot in Syria's no man's land?" featured on Thomson's personal *Channel 4* blog describes a tale of violence on both sides, with attempts to interview belligerents on both sides of the Syrian conflict, very uncharacteristic of Western and particularly British media coverage. Thomson's narrative describes what appears to be a bifurcation between "rebel" forces, stating that while organized fighters that appear to solely commit to fighting the Syrian Army, there appears to be a more insidious "third party" involved, a third party implicated by Thomson as having intentionally led him and his team into a deadly trap. This is a narrative that corroborates statements made by the Syrian government itself, as well as independent geopolitical analysts from around the world - that there exists a substantial third party, consisting of foreign mercenaries and sectarian extremists carrying out the bulk of the violence and atrocities. Thomson describes his ordeal after accompanying UN monitors out to "Free Syrian Army" held territory:

We decide to ask for an escort out the safe way we came in. Both sides, both checkpoints will remember our vehicle. Suddenly four men in a black car beckon us to follow. We move out behind. We are led another route. Led in fact, straight into a free-fire zone. Told by the Free Syrian Army to follow a road that was blocked off in the middle of no-man's-land. At that point there was the crack of a bullet and one of the slower three-point turns I've experienced. We screamed off into the nearest side street for cover. Another dead-end. There was no option but to drive back out onto the sniping ground and floor it back to the road we'd been led in on. Predictably the black car was there which had led us to the trap. They roared off as soon as we re-appeared. I'm quite clear the rebels deliberately set us up to be shot by the Syrian Army. Dead journos are bad for Damascus. In a war where they slit the throats of toddlers back to the spine, what's the big deal in sending a van full of journalists into the killing zone? It was nothing personal. [34]

The obvious question that comes to mind upon reading Thomson's account, is that if rebels are willing kill foreign journalists for propaganda value just to blame the deaths on the Syrian government, why wouldn't they kill men, women and children to blame on the Syrian government as well? Perhaps the most duplicitous case of media manipulation in Syria was uncovered by French journalist Thierry Meyssan, in his June, 2012 article, NATO Preparing Vast disinformation campaign, where an intelligence operation aiming to replace Syrian state TV broadcasts with fabricated footage filmed on sound stages in Doha & Riyadh is described:

---

[33] I saw massacre of children, says defecting Syrian air force officer, The Guardian, June 02, 2012
[34] Set up to be shot in Syria's no man's land? Channel 4 News, June 8, 2012

In a few days, perhaps as early as Friday, June 15, at noon, the Syrians wanting to watch their national TV stations will see them replaced on their screens by TV programs created by the CIA. Studio-shot images will show massacres that are blamed on the Syrian Government, people demonstrating, ministers and generals resigning from their posts, President Al-Assad fleeing, the rebels gathering in the big city centers, and a new government installing itself in the presidential palace. This operation of disinformation, directly managed from Washington by Ben Rhodes, the US deputy national security adviser for strategic communication, aims at demoralizing the Syrians in order to pave the way for a coup d'etat. NATO, discontent about the double veto of Russia and China, will thus succeed in conquering Syria without attacking the country illegally. Whichever judgment you might have formed on the actual events in Syria, a coup d'etat will end all hopes of democratization.

The Arab League has officially asked the satellite operators Arabsat and Nilesat to stop broadcasting Syrian media, either public or private (Syria TV, Al-Ekbariya, Ad-Dounia, Cham TV, etc.) A precedent already exists because the Arab League had managed to censure Libyan TV in order to keep the leaders of the Jamahiriya from communicating with their people. There is no Hertz network in Syria, where TV works exclusively with satellites. The cut, however, will not leave the screens black. Actually, this public decision is only the tip of the iceberg. According to our information several international meetings were organized during the past week to coordinate the disinformation campaign. The first two were technical meetings, held in Doha (Qatar); the third was a political meeting and took place in Riyadh (Saudi Arabia). The first meeting assembled PSYOP officers, embedded in the satellite TV channels of Al-Arabiya, Al-Jazeera, BBC, CNN, Fox, France 24, Future TV and MTV. It is known that since 1998, the officers of the US Army Psychological Operations Unit (PSYOP) have been incorporated in CNN. Since then this practice has been extended by NATO to other strategic media as well.

They fabricated false information in advance, on the basis of a "story-telling" script devised by Ben Rhodes's team at the White House. A procedure of reciprocal validation was installed, with each media quoting the lies of the other media to render them plausible for TV spectators. The participants also decided not only to requisition the TV channels of the CIA for Syria and Lebanon (Barada, Future TV, MTV, Orient News, Syria Chaab, Syria Alghad) but also about 40 religious Wahhabi TV channels to call for confessional massacres to the cry of "Christians to Beyrouth, Alawites into the grave!" In 2011, France 24 served as information ministry for the Libyan CNT, according to a signed contract. During the battle of Tripoli, NATO produced fake studio films, then transmitted them via Al-Jazeera and Al-Arabiya, showing phantom images of Libyan rebels on the central square of the capital city, while in reality they were still far away. As a consequence, the inhabitants of Tripoli were persuaded that the war was lost and gave up all resistance. Nowadays the media do not only support a war, they produce it themselves. [35]

Meyssan's groundbreaking report provides valuable insight into the role of the mainstream media and its capacity to propagate an entirely fictitious narrative in support of militant foreign policy aimed at toppling governments in non-compliant

---

[35] NATO preparing vast disinformation campaign, VoltaireNet, June 11, 2012

states. Due to increased calls to satellite operators by the Arab League requesting the Nilesat and Arabsat satellites stop broadcasting Syrian TV channels, the Syrian government accused groups of trying to mute the voice of the Syrian people and succeeded in halting the operation.[36] In late June 2012, Syrian rebels attacked and killed seven employees (including three journalists) at the Syrian *al-Ikhbaryia* Satellite Channel some 20 kilometers south of Damascus.[37] Rebels destroyed the studios with explosives, in an attack seen as an extension of the decision taken by the European Union on the previous day to impose sanctions on Syrian radio and television organizations. Undoubtedly, had Syrian President Bashar al-Assad's forces kidnapped and murdered journalists sympathetic to the West's narrative - relentless accusations of "crimes against humanity," referrals to the West's myriad of "international institutions," and self-proclaimed international arbiters would have followed. However, the perpetrators are instead terrorists receiving NATO backing, in an attack celebrated rather than condemned by the Western press, with *Reuters* describing the incident as "one of the boldest attacks yet on a symbol of the authoritarian state." [38] Journalist Thierry Meyssan reported from the scene of the destroyed studios, and was quoted as stating:

In the media war that takes place around Syria, you're probably wondering who is telling the truth. In the background, there are those who say that this country is the subject of an internal revolution and a terrible repression, and those who say instead that this country is attacked by foreign powers who have sent in armies of mercenaries and sophisticated commandos who engage in destruction of infrastructure and targeted assassinations. To understand what is happening, you must remember the propaganda system. Propaganda consists of intoxication from one side of the story giving you false information, and on the other side, you are prevented from receiving conflicting information. For this to occur, the contradictory media must be censored and destroyed.

In the midst of an unfettered media war, hackers allegedly working independently inside Syria have hacked Western media outlets and agencies such as *Al-Jazeera* in an attempt to counter the dominant media narrative. The prominent hacker-ring known as the Syrian Electronic Army has boldly denounced *Al-Jazeera* for broadcasting "false and fabricated news to ignite sedition among the people of Syria to achieve the goals of Washington and Tel Aviv," culminating in targeted cyber attacks on *Al-Jazeera's* "Syria Live Blog", which provides ongoing coverage of the unrest, and *Al-Jazeera's* 'Stream' *Twitter* account.[39] In an attack conducted in early July 2012, hackers gained access to the *Twitter* account and began sending out stories published by the alternative media, including videos allegedly depicting members of the opposition torturing, executing, and beheading Syrian military personnel and civilians on the basis of being religious minorities and Assad loyalists. In a recent interview conducted by a journalist from the Huffington Post, the anonymous leader of the Syrian Electronic Army claims his group operates

---

[36] News Analysis: Syria's Assad faces full war, XinhuaNet, June 28, 2012
[37] Attack Destroys Pro-Government TV Station Near Damascus, The New York Times, June 27, 2012
[38] Rebels storm Pro-Assad Syrian TV channel, Reuters, June 27, 2012
[39] Pro-government hactivists deface Al Jazeera coverage of Syrian violence, Ars Technica, Jan. 30, 2012

independently of the Syrian government stating, "We are not supported by anyone – we started this work since 15 March 2011 when we have seen a large numbers of terrorists spread around our country – so we decided to defend our country." [40]

On July 13th, 2012, over 100 people were slaughtered in the village of Tremseh, a village of 11,000 people about 22 miles northwest of Hama. Activists reported the Syrian government's use of artillery, tanks and helicopters, insinuating that state forces were behind the massacre. Upon the initial first reports issued by media outlets, the United States' UN Ambassador Susan Rice posted on her *Twitter* account, "Reports of Traymseh massacre are nightmarish – dramatically illustrate the need for binding UNSC measures on Syria."

Ambassador Rice scorned the Syrian state and threatened its government with further UN Resolutions prior to the arrival of any UN monitoring personnel to the area, before any semblance of an investigation had been conducted - even prior to any photography or video surfacing. This immediate accusation of state forces reflects the deceit and fraudulence of US leadership and the current state of international justice under the International Criminal Court, an organization only willing to indict those unfriendly to the private geopolitical and geo-economic objectives of Western capitals. In Tremseh, eyewitness accounts brought forth by *Al-Jazeera* claim government troops opened fire in retaliation, after the FSA attacked a neighboring Alawite village. Syria's *SANA News* reported the capture of 4 heavily armed non-Syrian Arab nationals who were ordered to attack military and police checkpoints and prevent state employees from going to work by sowing chaos.[41] Following the events in Tremseh, Syrian military forces on the scene seized an opposition weapons cache stocked with machine guns, sniper rifles, RPG launchers, mortars, explosive devices, gas masks, binoculars, satellite wireless devices, video cameras, large amounts of gunpowder, TNT templates, and highly explosive C4 material.[42]

The *New York Times'* July 14, 2012 article titled, "Details of a Battle Challenge Reports of a Syrian Massacre," claims that reports of a massacre in Tremseh were more accurately clashes between the heavily armed Syrian military and local opposition fighters wielding light weapons, with the latter bearing the majority of casualties. There were reportedly no women among the dead in Tremseh, while a list published by the Syrian National Council, cites that casualties were men between 19 and 36. Tremseh had allegedly been a regional base of operations for 200 to 300 militant fighters for a period of 20 days prior to the outbreak of violence. The *New York Times* Report further states:

After the high toll was announced from Tremseh, as was the case with Houla and other similar episodes, Western leaders lined up to condemn the mass killings of civilians. Col. Riad al-Assad, based in Turkey as the ostensible leader of the loose

---

[40] Syrian Electronic Army Leader: Cyber-War to Continue Against Those "Distorting the Truth About Syria," The Huffington Post, April 25, 2012

[41] Four Terrorists from al-Treimseh: Gunmen Were Ordered to Spread Across the Town Before Army Forces Entered It, SANA News, July 13, 2012

[42] The Armed Forces Carry out "Qualitative Operation" in al-Treismeh and Causes Heavy Losses among Terrorists, SANA News, July 13, 2012

coalition of fighters called the Free Syrian Army, told the Arabic television network Al Jazeera on Thursday that there had been no opposition fighters in the town. Although what actually happened in Tremseh remains murky, the evidence available suggested that events on Thursday more closely followed the Syrian government account. But Syrian officials colored that account with their usual terminology of blaming "foreign terrorist gangs" for all violence. The government said the Syrian Army had inflicted "heavy losses" on the "terrorists." [43]

Defections of members of the Syrian government holding high positions were few and far between throughout the crisis, only after the seventeenth month of the conflict were notable defections reported. One such senior official, Nawaf Fares, a former security chief and Syria's ambassador to Iraq now harbored in Qatar, dramatically defected by publishing a video message urging others to follow his example. In an interview with the *Telegraph*, Fares admits that Jihadi units that he himself helped Damascus send to fight the American occupation in neighboring Iraq were involved in the string of deadly suicide bomb attacks in Syria.[44] However, Fares accuses the Syrian government itself of orchestrating false flag terrorist attacks in the form of suicide bombings on its own government buildings in an attempt to incriminate rebel forces. Conflicting reports published by mainstream outlets confirm that foreign Al Qaeda aligned fighters have independently crossed into Syria, simply noting headlines such as "Al Qaeda head calls for fall of Assad" (*AP*), "Top US official: Al Qaeda in Iraq joining fight against Syria's Assad" (*McClatchy*), and "Al Qaeda's Zawahiri calls for war to oust Syria's Assad" (*AP*). Such headlines illustrate the absurdity of Fares' claims of President Bashar al-Assad "collaborating" with Al Qaeda in a conspiracy to accuse opposition forces for the ensuing atrocities.

Not only did Fares fail to provide any evidence that "Al Qaeda" has coordinated its bombing campaigns with Syrian security forces, but his claim directly contradicts months of reporting, such as Reuters' April 2012 exposé covering the Free Syrian Army's "tactical switch" to terrorist bombings in the face of superior military weapons and tactics employed by government security forces. The article explained that Syrian extremists who had honed their skills fighting US and British troops in Iraq had joined the ranks of the FSA to employ their bomb-making abilities against, not in collaboration with, the Syrian government. Nawaf Fares comes across as an exaggerating opportunist, so overly eager to play his role that he has tripped over himself and found both feet lodged firmly in his mouth. Fares abandoned a "regime" he finds unbearable, which he claims supported "Jihadi units" carrying out a terrorist bombing campaign against its own people, only to join a militant organization that has demonstratively and admittedly carried out bombing campaigns against the Syrian people. In a timely piece, the *Telegraph* reports that extremist fighters attempting to found Islamic caliphates have been operating openly in some areas of Idlib and Aleppo provinces that straddle the borders of Turkey and Iraq, where Al Qaeda's flags have been seen flying:

---

[43] Details of a Battle Challenge Reports of a Syrian Massacre, The New York Times' July 14, 2012
[44] Exclusive interview: why I defected from Bashar al-Assad's regime, by former diplomat Nawaf Fares, The Telegraph, July 14, 2012

"An al Qaeda group led by a man who called himself Abu Saddiq took control in Der Tezzeh," said one FSA rebel speaking on condition of anonymity. "I was a member of the Revolution Council there. Suddenly there was a new way of thinking. Abu Saddiq was installed as the 'Emir', or 'Prince' of the area for three months. I was told to put my hand on the Koran and to obey him. "He wanted to build a religious country. He did not want democracy but a religious leader in power. He wanted to use suicide bombers as a way of fighting government troops in the area." [45]

Just as in Libya, where former officials under Gaddafi embraced the opposition National Transition Council, it remains highly plausible that the defection of senior officials in Syria is motivated by those representatives receiving greater benefits and positions in the future by cooperating with the internationally recognized Syrian National Council opposition party. While the Syrian National Council is far from the only opposition group, its representatives and spokespeople are the most acknowledged due to their acquiescence and deep connections with Western think-thanks and policy makers, prompting British Foreign Minister William Hague to declare:

"I will meet leaders of the Syrian National Council in a few minutes' time ... We, in common with other nations, will now treat them and recognize them as a legitimate representative of the Syrian people." [46]

Journalist Charlie Skelton's July 2012 exposé, "The Syrian opposition: who's doing the talking?" published in the *Guardian*, details the intimate connections between senior members of the Syrian National Council who have been present at private gatherings such as the annual meetings conducted by the Bilderberg Group, and the West's most prestigious policy institutions and think-tanks.[47] One such individual is French-Syrian academic Bassma Kodmani, a senior official spokesperson for the Syrian National Council who fled Syria with her family at age ten following 1967's Six-Day War. Kodmani has since settled between London, Paris, and Egypt, where she led the Governance and International Cooperation program for the Middle East and North Africa at the Ford Foundation. Bassma Kodmani was installed as executive director of a research initiative established by the US-based Council on Foreign Relations, the Arab Reform Initiative (ARI), in September 2005, an institute aimed at promoting "reform and democratization in the Arab world." More specifically, the ARI was founded by a subgroup of senior diplomats, intelligence officers and financiers within the Council on Foreign Relations' "US/Middle East Project," chaired by former US National Security Advisor Brent Scowcroft. Accordingly, Kodmani is research director at the Académie Diplomatique Internationale, headed by Jean-Claude Cousseran, former head of the French intelligence service Direction Générale de la Sécurité Extérieure.

In February 2012, she was subjected to controversy for previously defending Israel on French television in 2008 stating, "We need Israel in the region." Although Kodmani warned she would later retract those statements, citing the opposition had

---

[45] Al-Qaeda tries to carve out a war for itself in Syria, The Telegraph, July 12, 2012

[46] Syria: Qatar calls for Arab force to impose peace - Friday 24 February, The Guardian, February 24, 2012

[47] The Syrian opposition: who's doing the talking? The Guardian, July 12, 2012

to rely on either the "greater militarization of local resistance or foreign intervention," claiming that "no dialogue with the ruling regime is possible. We can only discuss how to move on to a different political system." [48] Kodmani would later be quoted by *AFP* stating, "The next step needs to be a resolution under Chapter VII, which allows for the use of all legitimate means, coercive means, embargo on arms, as well as the use of force to oblige the regime to comply." Willingness to call for foreign military intervention appears to be a demanding requisite of Syrian National Council officials, such as Ausama Monajed, who is described on the SNC's website as being "widely quoted and interviewed in prestigious international media outlets including the *Wall Street Journal, New York Times*, The *Washington Post, Los Angeles Times, Foreign Policy Magazine, USA Today*," and others.

Monajed's July 2012 op-ed in the *Huffington Post* titled, "The Price of Apathy: Why the World Must Intervene in Syria," argued that the international community "has a moral obligation to help foster a viable resistance by establishing safe zones from which opposition forces can train, re-arm and seek refuge and medial assistance." [49] This description is identical to the Brooking Institution's March 2012 Memo, "Saving Syria: Assessing Options for Regime Change." Monajed is the founder and director of a pro-opposition satellite channel, *Barada Television*, and the former director of public relations with the Movement for Justice and Development (MJD), which received as much as $6 million from the US State Department and others since 2006, as reported by the *Washington Post*.[50] Monajed was a panelist for US-based Chatham House's 2009 event "Envisioning Syria's Political Future," along with Wissam Tarif, director of Madrid-based Syrian human rights group INSAN and SNC representative Radwan Ziadeh, a senior fellow at National Council and senior fellow at the federally funded US-based think-tank, the US Institute of Peace. In February 2012, Ziadeh joined Elizabeth Cheney, Karl Rove, James Woolsey, and others in calling for foreign intervention and economic sanctions against Syria through an open letter to President Obama.

The longstanding political and institutional support given to senior Syrian National Council officials demonstrates the disingenuous nature of leading figures within Syria's political opposition, who have been shaped by the privileged lives they've enjoyed in the West. While the political system under the Ba'ath Party is not without its shortcomings, the mere insinuation that a group of long-exiled, Western-educated Syrian academics should be recognized as "the legitimate representatives of the Syrian people" as advocated by British Foreign Minister William Hague and others, is nothing sort of a decisive mockery of the touted democratic principles these individuals and institutions claim to represent. In response to journalist Charlie Skelton's investigative piece published in the *Guardian*, the publications' own "diplomatic editor" Julian Borger responded with, "US manipulation of news from Syria is a red herring," a slander piece entirely reliant on branding Skelton a "conspiracy theorist." While Borger fails to critically assess any of the findings

---

[48] Syria's opposition concerned about independent armed rebel groups, The Christian Science Monitor, Janurary 27, 2012

[49] The Price of Apathy: Why the World Must Intervene in Syria, The Huffington Post, July 07, 2012

[50] U.S. secretly backed Syrian opposition groups, cables released by WikiLeaks show, The Washington Post, April 18, 2011

addressed in Skelton's article, he familiarly berates the author with tired insinuations of belief in "shadowy forces," in a manner typical of academic elitism and editorial condescension. Borger associates Skelton with historian and academic Webster Tarpley, and attempts to discredit them on the basis of questioning the official account of events on September 11th, 2001, before trumpeting the dominant narrative in Syria – that an oppressive government is remorselessly carried out a slaughter – and calling on the skewed International Criminal Court to investigate the situation.[51]

If these exhausted rebuttals are indicative of anything, it is that those individuals, intellectuals, academics, analysts, experts, commentators and news outlets are unwilling to address and seriously acknowledge the enormous discrepancies embedded within the dominate narrative of events in Syria. Their musings reflect their own personal weakness, conceit, and dishonesty. Undoubtedly, the conduct of the corporate news media in collaboration with compromised NGOs, front groups for Western intelligence, and the United Nations, constitutes a brazen attempt to sabotage a sovereign nation by methodically presenting a deeply dishonest and recycled narrative to the world. The media war being waged on Syria has been a vital component of the conflict, perhaps being the only means of publically legitimizing the opposition in an effort to topple the Syrian government. While some of the witness accounts coming from Syria may hold validity, the inconsistencies of those testimonies and the way in which organizations like the United Nations obscure such accounts with blanketing confidentiality only serve to further suspicions of fabrication and duplicity at the institutional level. As more and more people begin to question the credibility and accuracy of mainstream news media, their coverage of events in Syria reflects not only a deeply flawed editorial policy, but also their commitment to fully aiding militaristic ventures at the expense of millions of lives around the world. While the alternative media struggles with its limitations and is not without its shortcomings, independent journalists and political analysts have succeeded in exposing the insidiousness and intellectual dishonesty of the dominant narrative in an attempt to question and critically assess what the world has been told about the Syrian crisis. It is only with editorial transparency, journalistic integrity, and simple honesty that such conflicts in the future may be similarly exposed and averted.

(July 15, 2012)

---

[51] US manipulation of news from Syria is a red herring, The Guardian, July 13, 2012

Chapter 3: The Prospect of Regional War

"Naturally the common people don't want war; neither in Russia, nor in England, nor in America, nor in Germany. That is understood. But after all, it is the leaders of the country who determine policy, and it is always a simple matter to drag the people along, whether it is a democracy, or a fascist dictatorship, or a parliament, or a communist dictatorship. Voice or no voice, the people can always be brought to the bidding of the leaders. That is easy. All you have to do is to tell them they are being attacked, and denounce the pacifists for lack of patriotism and exposing the country to danger. It works the same in any country."

Hermann Göring

President of the German Reichstag

After a vicious decade of unpalatable war and occupation in the Middle East, the prospect of the Syrian crisis intensifying into larger regional conflict is an alarming possibility. Such a war would be propagated by manipulating sectarian divisions in an effort to sow chaos and trigger the collapse of the Assad government, thus threatening the foundations of secular nationalism in Syria and inciting tensions with Bashar-al Assad's closest diplomatic ally, Iran. As the United States and its allies attempt to destabilize Syria, the simultaneous isolation of Iran through economic sanctions, and the increasing American military presence in the Persian Gulf signifies a continued proclivity for war and foreign entanglement. From Saudi Arabia to Turkey, the emerging Islamic powers allied with the United States have worked in tandem to assist the militant Syrian insurgency, motivated ideologically by aspirations of halting the expansion of Shi'a identity, and their own ambitions of regional hegemony. As Israel continues to assert its right to preemptively strike Iran, Tel Aviv views the toppling of Damascus as a means of extinguishing the critical conduit between Tehran and Hezbollah, the political and militant Shi'a organization centered in Southern Lebanon, in a bid to isolate the Palestinian resistance. As Syrian rebel fighters mount further pressure on the Assad government, it must be remembered, that the road to Tehran goes through Damascus.

The pages of the 2010 US Military Special Forces' Unconventional Warfare Manual offer further insight into the insurrectionary nature of the Syrian conflict. A publication aimed at defining unconventional warfare tactics, the manual serves as a blueprint for decades of illegally conducted clandestine operations carried out without the approval of the US Congress. The document illustrates the sheer impunity with which the United States conducts its foreign policy, aimed at illegally interfering in the affairs of foreign nations in order to subvert and destabilize them in the name of furthering American interests:

The Commander, United States Special Operations Command (USSOCOM), defines [Unconventional Warfare] UW as activities conducted to enable a resistance movement or insurgency to coerce, disrupt, or overthrow a government or occupying power by operating through or with an underground, auxiliary, and guerrilla force in a denied area. The intent of U.S. [Unconventional Warfare] UW efforts is to exploit a hostile power's political, military, economic, and psychological vulnerabilities by developing and sustaining resistance forces to accomplish U.S. strategic objectives. For the foreseeable future, U.S. forces will predominantly engage in irregular warfare (IW) operations.[1]

The targets of the above mentioned irregular warfare operations are those sovereign states that have been historically unwilling to align themselves with American diplomatic and economic interests. These covert operations are meticulously orchestrated and conducted in phases; beginning with psychologically influencing targeted populations by

Subsequently, targeted nations are infiltrated to provide training and equipment to dissident groups, until a political transition is forcibly imposed:*Figure 1-3 Phases of Unconventional Warfare*

PHASE I: Preparation

Resistance and external sponsors conduct psychological preparation to unify population against established government or occupying power and prepare population to accept U.S. support.

PHASE II: Initial Contact

USG [United States Government] agencies coordinate with allied government-in-exile or resistance leadership for desired U.S. support.

PHASE III: Infiltration

SF [Special Forces] team infiltrates operational area, establishes communications with its base, and contacts resistance organization.

PHASE IV: Organization

SF [Special Forces] team organizes, trains, and equips resistance cadre. Emphasis is on developing infrastructure.

PHASE V: Buildup

SF [Special Forces] team assist cadre with expansion into an effective resistance organization. Limited combat operations may be conducted, but emphasis remains on development.

PHASE VI: Employment

UW [Unconventional Warfare] forces conduct combat operations until linkup with conventional forces or end hostilities.

PHASE VII: Transition

UW [Unconventional Warfare] forces revert to national control, shifting to regular forces or demobilizing.

The contents of the manual constitute unrestrained disregard for the principles of international law, national sovereignty, and the preparedness or political desire for change in those targeted nations. While the mainstream media emphasized the "spontaneity" of political revolt in the Arab World, the contents of the 2010 US

---

[1] Special Forces Unconventional Warfare, Department of US Army, November 2010

Military Special Forces' Unconventional Warfare Manual provide incredible clarity into the insurrectionary nature of resistance forces operating in target nations. One such notable section itemizes the "structure of an insurgency or resistance movement," pedantically detailing the stages of destabilization, from "underground activities" to "guerilla actions," in an attempt to undermine the legitimacy of target governments and ultimately topple them:

Figure 2-2. Structure of an insurgency or resistance movement

• *Dissatisfaction with Political, Economic, Social, Administrative, and Other Conditions; National Aspiration (Independence) or Desire for Ideological and Other Changes*

• *Creating an Atmosphere of Wider Discontent Through Propaganda and Political and Psychological Effects to Discredit the Government*

• *Agitation; Creation of Favorable Public Opinion (Advocating National Cause); Creation of Distrust of Established Institution*

• *Increased Agitation, Unrest, and Disaffection; Infiltration of Administration, Police, Military, and National Organizations, Boycotts, Slowdowns, and Strikes*

• *Infiltration of Foreign Organizers and Advisors and Foreign Propaganda, Material, Money, Weapons, and Equipment*

• *Recruitment and Training of Resistance Cadres*

• *Penetration into Labour Unions, Student and National Organizations and all Parts of Society*

• *Spreading of Subversive Organizations into All Sectors of Life of a Country*

• *Establishment of National Front Organizations and Liberation Movements; Appeal to Foreign Sympathizers*

• *Expansion of Front Organizations*

• *Intensification of Propaganda; Psychological Perpetration of Population for Rebellion*

• *Overt and Covert Pressures Against Government (Strikes, Riots, and Disorder)*

• *Increased Underground Activities to Demonstrate Strength of Resistance Organization and Weakness of Government*

• *Intense Sapping of Morale (Government, Administration, Police, Military)*

• *Increased Political Violence and Sabotage*

• *Minor Guerrilla Actions*

• *Large-Scale Guerilla Actions*

In the Syrian context, the "architecture of resistance" described by the 2010 Unconventional Warfare Manual mirrors every aspect of the uprising, from psychological operations conducted on targeted populations and the influx of arms and material goods, to the conduct of the insurgent fighters, who have incrementally increased the scale of their operations against the Syrian state to warrant labeling their conduct as "Large Scale Guerilla Actions". At minimum, the contents of the US Military document constitute nothing short of an admission that the United States advocates state-sponsored terrorism to achieve its foreign policy objectives of toppling foreign states. While senior US officials and diplomats publically tout democratic principles, Washington's "irregular warfare" operations place much emphasis on ensuring small militant factions forcibly legitimize themselves in the eyes of the population:

"In almost every scenario, resistance movements face a population with an active minority supporting the government and an equally small militant faction supporting the resistance movement. For the resistance to succeed, it must convince the uncommitted middle population…to accept it as a legitimate entity. A passive population is sometimes all a well-supported insurgency needs to seize political power."

In an age where the "War on Terror" is used as a pretext to militarily intervene and occupy sovereign states, it must not be forgotten that such disastrous tactics of "irregular warfare" were used to fund coalitions of fighters known as the Mujaheddin – later known as "al-Qaeda" – an organization whose dubious origins can be traced back to policy initiatives theorized by former Secretary of Defense Robert Gates and former National Security Adviser Zbigniew Brzezinski during the Soviet-Afghan war in in the late 1970's and throughout the 1980's.[2] Contrary to popular belief, the funding and support of fanatic militant groups did not begin after the Soviet invasion, but rather, several years prior to it. In the 1980's, the Mujaheddin were publically portrayed as heroes and freedom fighters, with Hollywood working to glamourize the armed resistance in Afghanistan. While the CIA fueled Afghanistan's decade-long war with the Soviet Union, many of those that fought in Afghanistan (particularly foreign fighters armed, trained, and brought in by the CIA) would go on to form some of the world's most notorious terrorist groups, many of which are listed today on the US and UK foreign terrorist organization lists. US intervention in Afghanistan by training and arming Afghanistan's Mujaheddin, along with Osama Bin Laden's Arab fighters, is one of the leading factors that led to the murderous and protracted decade-long war, which would formally establish al-Qaeda, an terrorist network that would continue to fight after the Soviets were expelled from Afghanistan, this time in Kosovo's bid for independence from Serbia in the late 1990's.

The al-Qaeda-trained Kosovo Liberation Army (KLA) militants garnered an armed Serbian response, which was then used by NATO as a pretext for intervention.

NATO's entry into the war led to the eventual carving up of the nation, while organizations such as the CIA were familiarly found to be propping up radical insurgent fighters. Al-Qaeda quickly became America's most notorious enemy, filling the void left by a collapsed Soviet Union and justifying Washington's unwarranted defense spending and expansion of enormous tactical holdings overseas throughout the 1990's. Al-Qaeda continued receiving covert support from US and British intelligence agencies with financial assistance from Saudi Arabia, as did many other extremist groups, which eventually began integrating with al-Qaeda across various regions of the world. These CIA-fostered terrorist groups include the Libyan Islamic Fighting Group (LIFG), which was created in Afghanistan with Libyan militants

---

[2] 'Blowback,' the Prequel, The Nation, October 25, 2001

previously armed and trained by the CIA to overthrow Muammar Gaddafi in the early 1980's. After several failed attempts to seize Libya by force, these fighters filtered back into Afghanistan to fight the occupying US. This time, the Afghans were no longer "gallant," but rather were portrayed as medieval, backwards, and in need of Western democracy and UN-sanctioned nation building. The Libyans for their part would continue fighting the US in Afghanistan, and when the US invaded Iraq in 2003, they would begin fighting US troops there as well.

While US forces occupied Afghanistan for more than a decade, with fighting reaching unprecedented levels, LIFG militants once again received military aid and diplomatic backing by NATO, along with full diplomatic recognition by the US State Department and the UK Foreign and Commonwealth Office as they rose up against Gaddafi in Libya, just as Afghanistan's Mujaheddin rallied against Soviet expansionism on behalf of Western foreign policy. This is a narrative that first saw these militants as heroes, then the world's most scorned villains for nearly a decade of war, before emerging once again as heroes. According to reports issued by the West Point Combating Terror Center, Libya's eastern region is considered to be one of the world's highest concentrations of terrorists, an area where Muammar Gaddafi had fought for nearly three decades to eliminate the region's foreign-backed militants, centered in the cities of Dernah and the epicenter of the NATO-backed rebellion, Benghazi.

The Muslim Brotherhood and various Sunni Islamist political factions that have usurped power in the wake of the US-engineered "Arab Spring" are the byproduct of a policy designed to undermine the governments of Iran and Syria, and Hezbollah operating in Lebanon, by widening sectarian conflict between Shi'a and Sunni Muslims. The creation of a united Sunni-front was noted by geopolitical analyst Dr. Webster Tarpley who has stated that the various new administrations resulting from these engineered revolutions "could then be used to support the fundamental US-UK strategy for the Middle East, which is to assemble a block of Arab and Sunni countries (notably Egypt, Saudi Arabia, the Gulf states, and Jordan) which, formed into a front with the participation of Israel, would collide with the Iranian Shiite front, including Syria, Hezbollah, Hamas, and various radical forces."

Confirming this analysis is a 2007 article published in the *New Yorker* by journalist Seymour Hersh, "The Redirection: Is the Administration's new policy benefiting our enemies in the war on terrorism?" Hersh's piece documents admissions that the US, Saudis, and Israelis are indeed allied (despite attempts by Saudi Arabia and influential Sunni organizations to portray themselves as "anti-Zionist"), and further confirms that the US has materially supported a regional network of extremist fighters and terrorists affiliated with al-Qaeda.[3] Hersh describes a policy shift that saw Washington collaborating with Riyadh to conduct clandestine operations intended to weaken Hezbollah in Lebanon, joining Saudi Arabia and Israel in a strategic embrace, largely because both countries perceive Iran as an existential threat. A principal component of this policy shift was the bolstering of Sunni extremist groups espousing a militant version of Islam against

---

[3] The Redirection, The New Yorker, March 05, 2007

Damascus, in an attempt to undermine Syria, Iran's primary conduit and platform of influence in the Arab world:

To undermine Iran, which is predominantly Shiite, the Bush Administration has decided, in effect, to reconfigure its priorities in the Middle East. In Lebanon, the Administration has cooperated with Saudi Arabia's government, which is Sunni, in clandestine operations that are intended to weaken Hezbollah, the Shiite organization that is backed by Iran. The U.S. has also taken part in clandestine operations aimed at Iran and its ally Syria. A by-product of these activities has been the bolstering of Sunni extremist groups that espouse a militant vision of Islam and are hostile to America and sympathetic to Al Qaeda. [4]

Hersh cites the key architects behind the policy shift toward clandestine operations as being former US Vice-President Dick Cheney, former Deputy National Security Advisor Elliott Abrams, former US Ambassador to Iraq Zalmay Khalilzad, and the infamous Prince Bandar bin Sultan, the former Saudi National-Security Advisor.

The importance of Prince Bandar (a close friend and business partner of George H.W. Bush, who genially designated him with the nickname, "Bandar Bush") in Washington's effort to undermine Tehran and its influence in the Middle East cannot be understated. Bandar, who served as the Ambassador to the United States for twenty-two years, was quoted by Hersh as saying, "We have two nightmares, for Iran to acquire the bomb and for the United States to attack Iran. I'd rather the Israelis bomb the Iranians, so we can blame them. If America does it, we will be blamed." During his tenure as Ambassador to the United States, Bandar developed close relationships with senior US officials, allied with the goal of halting the expansion of Shi'a political power and influence in the Middle East. Hersh highlights how Saudi officials used their enormous wealth as financial leverage against the feared emergence of the religious minority Shi'a, who are a majority in Iran, Iraq, Bahrain, and Lebanon, and are widely viewed as heretics by Sunnis. For the allied powers in Tel Aviv, Riyadh, and Washington, militant Sunni radicals are lesser enemies of the West in contrast to the geopolitical emergence of a "Shiite crescent." This is an ironic stance for the United States to adopt while spearheading war against Iraq, where most cases of insurgent violence US forces dealt with came from militant Sunni forces. Former US President George Bush accused Iran and Syria of allowing terrorists to move in and out of their territories to provide material support to resistance fighters pitted against the American occupation in Iraq. The Bush Administration's own failures in planning and executing their program in Iraq were justified as the result of Iranian interference. In an attempt to build a case against Iran interfering in Iraq, US military personnel arrested and interrogated hundred of Iranians in Iraq, many of whom were providing humanitarian aid and medical assistance to war-torn Iraq:

Flynt Leverett, a former Bush Administration National Security Council official, told me that "there is nothing coincidental or ironic" about the new strategy with regard to Iraq. "The Administration is trying to make a case that Iran is more dangerous and

---

[4] Ibid

more provocative than the Sunni insurgents to American interests in Iraq, when—if you look at the actual casualty numbers—the punishment inflicted on America by the Sunnis is greater by an order of magnitude," Leverett said. "This is all part of the campaign of provocative steps to increase the pressure on Iran. The idea is that at some point the Iranians will respond and then the Administration will have an open door to strike at them." [5]

Hersh's article also describes in great detail the role of Saad Hariri, the former Lebanese Prime Minister who worked closely with Saudi Arabia and the United States to create a safe haven for terrorist organizations on Lebanese soil, who have been instrumental in destabilizing neighboring Syria:

The Saudi government, with Washington's approval, would provide funds and logistical aid to weaken the government of President Bashar Assad, of Syria. The Israelis believe that putting such pressure on the Assad government will make it more conciliatory and open to negotiations. Syria is a major conduit of arms to Hezbollah. The Saudi government is also at odds with the Syrians over the assassination of Rafik Hariri, the former Lebanese Prime Minister, in Beirut in 2005, for which it believes the Assad government was responsible. Hariri, a billionaire Sunni, was closely associated with the Saudi regime and with Prince Bandar. [6]

The Muslim Brotherhood is often portrayed as being anti-Israeli, anti-American, and anti-Western in general. In reality, Hersh's 2007 report makes clear that the Brotherhood was the vehicle of choice for the US, Israeli, and Saudi elite aimed at halting Shi'a expansionism; an organization that has long received backing and direct funding not only in Syria, but in Egypt as well. The Muslim Brotherhood's rank and file surely believes in what they are being told by their leaders, who have proven themselves to be professional demagogues peddling anti-Israeli and anti-American rhetoric solely for public consumption while being fully complicit in the West's designs against the Arab World. Hersh reports that a supporter of the Lebanese Hariri faction met Dick Cheney in Washington and personally relayed the priority of using the Muslim Brotherhood in Syria in any move against the ruling government:

[Walid] Jumblatt then told me that he had met with Vice-President Cheney in Washington last fall to discuss, among other issues, the possibility of undermining Assad. He and his colleagues advised Cheney that, if the United States does try to move against Syria, members of the Syrian Muslim Brotherhood would be 'the ones to talk to,' Jumblatt said.

Hersh's exposé detailed how backing by the United States and Saudi Arabia had begun benefiting the Brotherhood since at least 2007:

There is evidence that the Administration's redirection strategy has already benefitted the Brotherhood. The Syrian National Salvation Front is a coalition of opposition groups whose principal members are a faction led by Abdul Halim Khaddam, a former Syrian Vice-President who defected in 2005, and the Brotherhood. A former high-ranking C.I.A. officer told me, "The Americans have provided both political and financial support. The Saudis are taking the lead with financial support,

---

[5] Ibid
[6] Ibid

but there is American involvement." He said that Khaddam, who now lives in Paris, was getting money from Saudi Arabia, with the knowledge of the White House. (In 2005, a delegation of the Front's members met with officials from the National Security Council, according to press reports.) A former White House official told me that the Saudis had provided members of the Front with travel documents. [7]

Indeed, the ploy described in incredible detail in 2007 has demonstrably come to fruition, not to protect against existential threats to the people of Saudi Arabia, Israel, or the United States, but against existential threats to their leadership's ambitions of regional hegemony:

Bandar and other Saudis have assured the White House that "they will keep a very close eye on the religious fundamentalists." Their message to us was "We've created this movement, and we can control it. It's not that we don't want the Salafis to throw bombs; it's who they throw them at—Hezbollah, Moqtada al-Sadr, Iran, and at the Syrians, if they continue to work with Hezbollah and Iran." [8]

Poetic Justice in the Persian Gulf

The enflaming of regional sectarian divisions holds enormous implications for the Middle East, particularly the prospect of "blowback" in the Kingdom. Saudi Arabia has a significant Shiite minority in its oil rich Eastern Province, and the House of Saud believes that Iranian operatives have been actively working with the local Shi'a population to destabilize the region. As the nations targeted for regime change and destabilization either falter or aggressively attempt to restore order in their own nations, the possibility of an authentic indigenous revolution is terrifying to those Arab nations who have uncompromisingly worked to destroy the Syrian state. The ultra-conservative ideological *Saudi Wahhabism* practiced in the Kingdom purges many common Muslim practices on the basis of being considered as impurities and innovations in Islam. While Riyadh has called for democracy and respect for human rights in Syria, the House of Saud presides over an absolutist state where political parties are prohibited and capital punishment by public beheading can be imposed as punishment for fornication, witchcraft, and apostasy from Islam.

Under a governance system reminiscent of medieval Europe, the Wahhabi ideology strictly forbids dissent as the House of Saud exerts control over the Salafist religious establishment to issue fatwas (a legal pronouncement in Islamic law) to legitimize their unchallenged authority. Because it is a major exporter of oil and a staunch ally of the United States, Washington has largely turned a blind eye to the glaring hypocrisies of Saudi absolutism, giving the regime free reign to violate principles that other nations are falsely accused of violating. In late February 2011, protests erupted in the Shi'a majority Bahrain, calling for greater political freedom and equality for the majority Shia population, as well as the downfall of the monarchy of King Hamad bin Isa Al Khalifa.[9] Ominously, Khalifa requested a Saudi-led contingent of the GCC's Peninsula Shield Force (PSF) to extinguish opposition protests under the auspices of the GCC's Peninsula Shield defense pact before

---

[7] Ibid

[8] Ibid

[9] Bahrain mourners call for end to monarchy, The Guardian, February 18, 2011

declaring martial law and a three-month state of emergency. Bahraini and Saudi Arabian forces unleashed a vicious offensive against unarmed civilian protesters in Manama's Pearl Square and have continued to exert excessive force according to reports issued by the Bahrain Independent Commission of Inquiry (BICI).[10]

As the situation escalated in Bahrain, the government blamed Iran for instigating unrest as the reactionary regime in Riyadh deliberately enflamed sectarian rhetoric in fear of its own Shi'a minority revolting, in order to instigate inter-religious strife which would reduce the likelihood of any uprising by the Sunni majority within Saudi Arabia.[11] Since February 2011, protesters regularly held demonstrations in Saudi Arabia, mainly in Qatif and Awamiyah in the eastern province, calling for the release of all political prisoners and freedom of expression. On March 5th, 2011, the Saudi Interior Ministry issued a statement prohibiting "all forms of demonstrations, marches or protests, and calls for them, because that contradicts the principles of the Islamic sharia, the values and traditions of Saudi society, and results in disturbing public order and harming public and private interests." [12] The February 2012 arrest and detention of prominent Shi'a Sheikh Nimr Baqr al-Nimr in Saudi Arabi's eastern province of al-Awamiyah fueled popular sentiments against the regime, prompting open dissent and rare displays of wider protest, spreading to Sunni areas in Hejaz, and even to Mecca and the political powerbase of Riyadh. Al-Nimr has allegedly been tortured for criticizing Saudi authorities for their treatment of the Shi'a minority and calling for secession of the oil-rich eastern province prior to predicting the overthrow of the government if repression continued.

In July 2012, CIA Director David Petraeus flew to Jeddah and met with Saudi King Abdullah bin Abdulaziz Al Saud, shortly after the monarch ordered the country's security forces to go on a state of high alert due to what he called a "turbulent situation" in the region.[13] Although no reports surfaced of what was discussed during the meeting, one would assume the pair conversed over issues such as Washington's concern over an internal power struggle within the royal family, the ailing health of King Abdullah, and the increasing violent crackdown on Shi'a activists and anti-government protestors. Deep splits within in the royal family became apparent as the several thousand princes and princesses began setting up their own coalitions to address chronic problems such as unemployment, corruption and inadequate housing, despite the enormous financial resources from oil exports.

The death of regime hardliner Prince Nayef bin Abdul Aziz in June 2010 exposed the fragility of transition in the Saudi Kingdom; Nayef headed the domestic security and intelligence apparatus and was known for cracking down on the security threat posed by Al Qaeda and its affiliates operating inside Saudi Arabia, a preeminent threat to the stability of the monarchy. Prior to his death, he introduced a welfare package to alleviate issues of youth unemployment in the country, which was perceived as an inadequate solution to an increasingly severe problem in the Kingdom. Nayef was seen as a figure that held de facto control over the Saudi state

---

[10] Bahraini regime forces attack 311 houses: al-Wefaq, PressTV, July 21, 2012
[11] Bahrain protesters join anti-government march in Manama, BBC, March 9, 2012
[12] CIA director meets Saudi king in Jeddah, PressTV, July 10, 2012
[13] Ibid

due to the ailing health of 89-year old King Abdullah, and was an aggressive opponent of both Iran and Hezbollah, whom he accused of intentionally undermining the Sunni population of Iraq and Lebanon. One of Nayef's foreign policy objectives aimed to topple Shi'a Iraqi leaders Muqtada al- Sadr, Ammar al-Hakim and Prime Minister Nuri al-Malki for their close ties to Tehran.

Since the 1979 Islamic Revolution in Iran, Arab monarchies in the Persian Gulf sought to increase their ties, perceiving Iran to be a threat to their interests. Saudi Arabia believes that the unrest in Bahrain and in its own Shi'a dominated eastern province has been bolstered by Iran's clerical establishment, viewing the religious minority as representing the interests of Tehran. Riyadh's intentions to establish a stronger economic union with Bahrain is likely motivated by Iran's territorial claims over the region and their opposition to the establishment of such a confederacy:

"In a reference to Iran's historical territorial claims over Bahrain, an Iranian parliamentarian lashed out against Saudi Arabia's plans: 'If it [Bahrain] is supposed to be annexed, it will go to the Islamic Republic not [the] al-Saud [family]'. In a more official response, Iranian Foreign Ministry spokesman Ramin Mehmanparast suggested, 'The crackdown on people, military and security intervention by neighboring countries like Saudi Arabia, and plans like the proposal for the formation of a union between Bahrain and Saudi Arabia are, in our view, ill-advised measures, which will deepen the crisis'. Given the stakes involved, Bahrain will remain a crucial strategic battleground between Saudi Arabia and Iran in the months ahead." [14]

While condemning and marginalizing its Shi'a population domestically, the Kingdom's airwaves have been dominated by fiery rhetoric from the Salafist religious establish calling for jihad against the Assad regime in Syria, going as far as formalizing a pay structure for members of the Free Syrian Army and other insurgents operating in Syria with cooperation from their Gulf allies. As dissident groups in neighboring Qatar issue nationwide calls demanding the ouster of Emir Sheikh Hamad bin Khalifa Al Thani and the dismantling of Qatar's domestic US base, the Kingdom is undoubtedly petrified by the prospect of an internal revolt at a time when around half the population is under 18-years old and the ageing upper echelons of the royal family are increasingly perceived to be repressive and reactionary.[15] In a country where the "showcase of reform" is the formation of an allegiance council to select the heir to the throne twice within an eight-month period, the Kingdom may well find itself paralyzed by the growing internal political movement calling for an end to the House of Saud. The hypocrisy of King Abdullah calling on Bashar al-Assad to implement genuine reform and "halt the killing machine," demonstrates the dishonesty of the Saudi line, as the Kingdom's support for sectarian insurgency in Syria constitutes nothing short of state-directed jihad:

The Saudis are driven by their fear that Iran could tilt the balance of power not only in the region, but within their own country. Saudi Arabia has a significant Shiite minority in its Eastern Province, a region of major oil fields; sectarian tensions are high

---

[14] Saudi Arabia-Bahrain union reflects Gulf rivalry, Asia Times Online, June 20, 2012
[15] Dissidents call for public protests against Doha regime, U.S. bases in Qatar, Tehran Times, July 24, 2012

in the province. The royal family believes that Iranian operatives, working with local Shiites, have been behind many terrorist attacks inside the kingdom, according to Vali Nasr. "Today, the only army capable of containing Iran"—the Iraqi Army—"has been destroyed by the United States. You're now dealing with an Iran that could be nuclear-capable and has a standing army of four hundred and fifty thousand soldiers." (Saudi Arabia has seventy-five thousand troops in its standing army.) Nasr went on, "The Saudis have considerable financial means, and have deep relations with the Muslim Brotherhood and the Salafis"—Sunni extremists who view Shiites as apostates. "The last time Iran was a threat, the Saudis were able to mobilize the worst kinds of Islamic radicals. Once you get them out of the box, you can't put them back." [16]

Saudi Arabia's participation in destabilizing Syria is seen as a means of ultimately diminishing the influence of Iran in the Arab world, and aiding the establishment of an absolutist, Sunni satellite-state in Damascus. Due to international embargoes on Iran, the Kingdom's oil production levels are at a thirty-year high and it can be safely expected that Saudi Arabia and its Gulf allies would militarily back Israel and the United States if they choose to strike Iran's nuclear facilities.[17] Riyadh would not likely be satisfied with regime change in Iran; they seek their own regional hegemony by weakening the Shi'a state entirely. The Kingdom would support insurgent movements aimed at capturing Tehran's resources and threatening the territorial integrity of the country along ethnic lines, encouraging Iran's Kurds in the northwest, Balochs in the southeast and Arabs in the west to take up arms in support of their own autonomy. As Riyadh desperately injects its tremendous financial resources into welfare programs and subsidies to appease the agitated population, the Kingdom is approaching a crossroads that may challenge the absolutist rule of the House of Saud. As the Kingdom and its Gulf allies move to enthusiastically support the uprising in Syria, historian and geopolitical analyst Dr. Webster Tarpley foreshadows instability for the monarchy, warning Riyadh's reactionary ruling class to examine the case of Louis Philippe Joseph d'Orléans, a member of ruling House of Bourbon dynasty, who enthusiastically supported the French Revolution, only to find himself eventually under the blade of the guillotine.

Turkey and the Kurdish Question

Under the direction of Prime Minister Recep Tayyip Erdoğan and Foreign Minister Ahmet Davutoğlu, Turkish foreign policy has aggressively shifted away from the touted "Zero Problems" policy, transforming into an intrusive spearhead ripping into the Syrian state. Turkey's close geographic proximity to Syria has given rise to arms trafficking, turning the Turkish-Syrian border into a flashpoint for insurgent fighters taking refuge with the full complicity of Ankara. The increasing militarization of Turkey's border with Syria serves as an uncomfortable indication of the conflict's severity, where match and tinder can meet at any moment with debilitating consequences for the region. In May 2012, the Council on Foreign Relations sponsored an Independent Task Force led by former US Secretary of State Madeleine Albright, former National Security Adviser Stephen J. Hadley, and twenty-five others, who issued a report entitled, "U.S.-Turkey Relations: A New Partnership."

---

[16] The Redirection, The New Yorker, March 05, 2007
[17] Saudi Arabia says kingdom pumping 10 million bpd, the most in 5 months, Al-Arabiya, May 8, 2012

[18] The document is written in the context of how Turkey can benefit the United States with respect to Syria and Iran, not without empty promises to entice Turkish leaders into falling on their swords for Western ambitions across the Middle East. The CFR's attempt to flesh out an improved alliance between the US and Turkey, claiming the new relationship would trump the potential for US cooperation with any BRICS nation (except perhaps India), serves as a patronizing political stunt attempting to fill Turkish leaders with delusions of grandeur, tempting them to lead the charge against Syria and Iran in exchange for Western support behind Ankara's ambitions of regional hegemony. In late July 2012, *Reuters* confirmed the existence of rebel base in Adana, a southern Turkish city roughly 100 km from the Syrian border, requested by Saudi Deputy Foreign Minister Prince Abdulaziz bin Abdullah al-Saud during an official visit. Adana is also home to a US-NATO base at Incirlik, confirming suspicions of direct covert American involvement. *Reuters*'s source in Qatar was quoted as saying:

"Three governments are supplying weapons: Turkey, Qatar and Saudi Arabia," said a Doha-based source. Ankara has officially denied supplying weapons. "All weaponry is Russian. The obvious reason is that these guys (the Syrian rebels) are trained to use Russian weapons, also because the Americans don't want their hands on it. All weapons are from the black market. The other way they get weapons is to steal them from the Syrian army. They raid weapons stores." The source added: "The Turks have been desperate to improve their weak surveillance, and have been begging Washington for drones and surveillance." The pleas appear to have failed. "So they have hired some private guys to come do the job."

The depreciation of Turkey's status to an acquiescent arm of the US Intelligence establishment may likely come at great cost to Prime Minister Erdoğan, as the collapse of the Syrian state could yield a closer collaboration between Syrian Kurdish rebels operating in northern Syria and Turkey's own Kurdish militant resistance, pushing the insurgency further into eastern Turkey and, consequently, destabilizing the country. The Kurdish minority in Turkey makes up more than a quarter of the total population and has fought a militant separatist campaign in the Kurdish region for decades led by the Kurdistan Workers' Party (PKK), who would pose an immediate threat to the domestic security of Turkey if bolstered by an influx of Syrian Kurdish rebels.

Kurdistan is a roughly defined geo-cultural region encompassing areas of eastern Turkey, northeastern Syria, northern Iraq and northwestern Iran, where nationalist organizations have historically fought for the establishment of an independent state and greater autonomy within existing national borders. Iraqi Kurdish leader Massoud Barzani of the autonomous Kurdistan Regional Government (KRG) in northern Iraq has proved to be an amenable candidate for the United States to use in manipulating Turkish policy. Barzani maintains control over Iraqi Kurdistan's rich oil fields, where the likes of ExxonMobil and Chevron have acquired a combined area of 1,124 square kilometers, much to the dismay of Iraq's Central government in

---

[18] U.S.-Turkey Relations, Council on Foreign Relations, May 2012

Baghdad, which views the deal with Barzani's provincial authority as bypassing Iraq's sovereignty.

The oil is intended to be exported onto international markets, and while Iraq and Turkey's Kirkuk-Ceyhan pipeline could be used as an exit point, a more attractive transportation route for the considerable oil and gas deposits in Kurdistan (containing between 3 and 6 trillion cubic meters of natural gas and 45 billion barrels of oil) would be the Syrian port city of Latakia, situated on the eastern Mediterranean. As Ankara is determined to expand its energy consumption to fuel its domestic economy, Turkey's Energy Minister Taner Yildiz has enthusiastically embraced economic cooperation with the Kurdistan Regional Government, despite Baghdad's affirmations of the provincial government illegally approving energy deals to export Kurdistani natural gas to Siyah Kalem, a Turkish engineering and construction company. For Ankara, Massoud Barzani is a strategic ally, as Turkish foreign policy toward Syria and Iraq converge. Iraq is Turkey's second largest trading partner, with more than half of Ankara's $12 billion trade being conducted with Barzani's KRG. Barzani is viewed not only as a business partner, but also as a vital figure who can leverage Turkey's problems with Kurdish militancy within its own borders by spearheading a new political track for the region's various Kurdish factions.

In April 2012, Barzani made an official visit to Washington to establish a US-Kurdistan Business Council to promote American investment in the region, meeting with President Barack Obama, Defense Secretary Leon Panetta, Deputy Secretary of State William Burns, Secretary of State Hillary Clinton and Vice President Joe Biden. Iraq's Shi'a Prime Minister Nouri al-Maliki has fallen out of favor with Washington and Turkey for deepening ties to Iran and for diplomatically siding with Bashar al-Assad's government. The United States originally backed Maliki assuming that a Shiite government in Iraq could work in Washington's favor to undermine the Sunni extremist circles that vigorously fought against American occupation, although this led to the bolstering of Shi'a radical militias under Maliki's watch. Unsurprisingly, Barzani espoused harsh rhetoric toward Iraq's central government upon returning from Washington:

He told al-Hayat, "Iraq is moving toward a catastrophe, a return to dictatorship", and that on his return to Arbil he would call a meeting of Iraqi leaders to "save" the country from Maliki and to seek "radical solutions." [19]

Undoubtedly, Barzani is referring to the prospect of Kurdish secession from Iraq, an attractive strategy for the United States and a move that Turkey would itself support under circumstances that benefit its own interests. Barzani has attempted to reconcile differences between various Kurdish groups by bribing factional leaders with Turkish money, even endeavoring to persuade Syrian Kurds to align with the anti-Assad opposition. Turkish PM Erdoğan met directly with Barzani in Istanbul, leading the charge against Maliki's administration in Baghdad in tandem with the Persian Gulf nations that have worked to systematically demolish the Syrian state, stating:

---

[19] US, Turkey and Iraqi Kurds join hands, Asia Times Online, April 24, 2012

"The basis of the political crisis in which Iraq finds itself is that Iraqi politicians seek to consolidate power and exclude others, rather than [follow] politics based on democratic and universal principles. It is a fact that behind the misperceptions that led to the accusations against Turkey by Prime Minister Maliki, who instigated the crisis in Iraq, this wrong understanding of politics can be found." [20]

Once again in step with the absolutist Gulf states, the underlying motive of a demonization of Iraq's government is the isolation of Iran by strangling its allies and promoting a relationship between Iraq's Kurdish and Sunni leadership, thereby undermining Maliki's administration in Baghdad. An interview with Hezbollah's leader Hassan Nasrallah conducted in 2007 alluded to the prospect of a geopolitical restructuring of the region along ethnic and sectarian lines:

Nasrallah said he believed that President Bush's goal was "the drawing of a new map for the region. They want the partition of Iraq. Iraq is not on the edge of a civil war—there is a civil war. There is ethnic and sectarian cleansing. The daily killing and displacement which is taking place in Iraq aims at achieving three Iraqi parts, which will be sectarian and ethnically pure as a prelude to the partition of Iraq. Within one or two years at the most, there will be total Sunni areas, total Shiite areas, and total Kurdish areas. Even in Baghdad, there is a fear that it might be divided into two areas, one Sunni and one Shiite." [21]

Ankara's reliance on emboldening Barzani's ambitions to lead an independent Kurdish entity, with Arbil as its capital in northern Iraq, comes with the hope that the KRG can play a central role in smothering Kurdish insurgents in eastern Turkey led by the militant Kurdistan Workers' Party (PKK), which uses northern Iraq as a primary base of operations. On a state visit to Ankara, Barzani addressed the issue of Kurdish militancy:

You won't get anywhere with weapons. The PKK should lay down its arms. I will not let the PKK prevail in northern Iraq ... If the PKK goes ahead with weapons, it will bear the consequences. [22]

Barzani has toed the Turkish line despite the fact that the PKK enjoys widespread sympathy among Kurds in northern Iraq, primarily because he believes having powerful friends with deep pockets in Ankara, Doha and Riyadh will empower him financially and politically. The reactionary Arab monarchies perceive Maliki's Iraq to be a meddlesome outpost of Iranian influence. They seek to add a Kurdish dimension to foreign policy directed at Syria, aiming to prevent the PKK from rekindling old alliances with Bashar al-Assad's government in Damascus. Barzani's success in persuading Syria's Kurds (who constitute about 10% of the country's population) to join the rebellion against Assad depends on supporting their separatist demands to oversee an autonomous Kurdish region in eastern Syria. Ankara's policy on Syria walks a delicate line and is fundamentally hypocritical in its support for Kurdish autonomy abroad while ruthlessly quelling movements holding similar aspirations domestically. Given the extent to which Ankara has made itself into a suppressor of

---

[20] Ibid

[21] The Redirection, The New Yorker, March 05, 2007

[22] US, Turkey and Iraqi Kurds join hands, Asia Times Online, April 24, 2012

domestic Kurdish nationalism, its support for Iraq's Kurdish population and other international factions may likely trigger high public resentment, leading to insurgent activity in Syria which would bleed into the Turkish state.

One case of misjudged economic development comes with an underlying political component that holds alarming consequences for local residents and areas of historical archaeological importance in Hasankeyf, a small village in southeastern Turkey. This is one of the oldest continuously inhabited human settlements with records dating back approximately 9,500 years. Ankara's State Hydraulic Works has pressed forward with the construction of the hydroelectric Ilisu Dam, which would cause immense ecological harm to the Tigris River valley by raising water levels and flooding nearby canyons that are currently dry. Although Turkey is among the world's highest potential geothermal energy providers, the construction of the Ilisu Dam in Hasankeyf would submerge the entire village with its population of three thousand residents and irreplaceable cultural heritage, despite the completed dam producing less than 2% of Turkey's total energy needs.[23] Ankara has openly declared that one of the main functions of the project is to drown out strongholds of the Kurdistan Workers' Party, whose militants operate from the mountainous Iraqi-Turkish border.[24] Both the governments in Syria and Iraq have condemned the project and raised grave concerns that Turkey's dam construction upstream will affect around 55,000 people living along the Tigris River in other nations. The destruction of a site containing artifacts from numerous ancient civilizations and the tomb of Iman Abdullah, thought to be a close relative of the Prophet Mohammad, will undoubtedly work to fan the flames of a Kurdish backlash into Turkey.[25]

As a result of Turkey's aggressive stance on Syria, Ankara may jeopardize its substantial trade relations and energy development projects with both Russia and China. The construction of Turkey's Mersin Akkuyu nuclear plant serves as Russia's largest foreign investment, estimated at $20 billion, and would help develop Ankara's energy sector as it moves toward advanced economic development.[26] Given the mutual benefits to both Ankara and Moscow from economic cooperation, the possibility of significantly reducing those ties is unlikely, unless Turkey militarily intervenes in Syria directly outside the mandate of the United Nations. Both parties have agreed to the South Stream pipeline project, to transport Russian natural gas to Europe by passing through Turkish territorial waters, with the trade volume between the two countries reaching $100 billion within five years. Considering Russia's significant investments into Turkish industry, communication services, banking institutions, and the establishment of a High Level Cooperation Council introduced by former Russian President Medvedev, Moscow may be willing to turn a blind eye to Turkish aggression to preserve its own interests by bringing the diplomatic and political stance of the two countries closer, not without vocal criticisms from the Russian Foreign Ministry. In late July, statements by Russian

---

[23] Turkey's Geothermal Energy Potential, Stanford University, February 2010
[24] Turkey's Hasankeyf dam can drown Kurds' hideaways, Asia Times Online, June 12, 2012
[25] Turkish history to sink to oblivion, Asia Times Online, September 08, 2010
[26] Turkey and Russia develop strategic alliance, Today's Taman, Janurary 29, 2012

Foreign Minister Sergei Lavrov were critical of Turkey, which allowed border
checkpoints with Syria to be captured by militants:

*"According to some information, these checkpoints were seized not by the Free
Syrian Army at all - whatever one thinks about it - but by groups directly linked with al
Qaeda," Lavrov said at a news conference with his Cypriot counterpart. "We are
double-checking this," said Lavrov, suggesting that Western nations should not rush to
celebrate territorial gains by opponents of President Bashar al-Assad's government. "If
such processes - the seizure of territory by terrorists - are supported by our partners,
then we would like to receive an answer to the question of what their position on Syria
is, what they are trying to achieve in that country," he said.* [27]

Despite cynicism from Moscow, chances are higher of Turkey being denied entry
into the Shanghai Cooperation Organization (SCO) for its belligerence in Syria than
the prospect of any substantial freezing in trade relations with Russia. Turkey was
granted dialogue partner status at the SCO's 2012 Beijing Summit, and has shifted
away from attempting to join the fledgling European Union with a renewed focus on
integration with the SCO.[28] Turkey's strategic geographic proximity makes it a
valuable trading partner and ally to Beijing, with their ambitions to develop the
energy potential of Central Asia by means of a "New Silk Road", bridging several
countries to connect China and Turkey. While cases of Turkish armed forces
attempting to interfere with Russian vessels delivering cargo to Syria would
unquestionably strain relations between the two countries, Ankara is actively
endangering its export trade to Russia, estimated at more than $1 billion.
Throughout the Syrian crisis, Turkey's irresponsible conduct as the ostensible
dagger of NATO has taken Ankara down an unproductive path of aggression,
enflaming tension with its allies and regional neighbors, and disenfranchising its
own elected officials. Among others, Refik Er-Yilmaz, legislator of the Republican
People's Party and member of the Turkish parliament, has lashed out against the
nation's border becoming a hub for "swarms of CIA and Mossad spies infiltrating into
Syria freely," criticizing Turkish foreign policy, calling it irrational and unsuccessful:

*He noted that local people in the province are getting agitated over the presence of
the strangers. Turkish police remain mute spectators as the spies carry various types of
identification, Er-Yimaz went on to say. He also accused the authorities of allowing
American and Israeli troopers on Turkish soil without any approval from the
parliament. Er-Yilmaz's comments came after the deputy of the Republican People's
Party, Osman Faruk Logoglu, on Monday blamed Turkey's ruling Justice and
Development Party for fomenting the unrest in Syria. Logoglu criticized the Turkish
government for aggravating the situation by sending military forces and vehicles
towards the Syrian border.* [29]

Ankara's readiness to host militants on their territory and hesitation to negotiate
with Damascus is fraught with high risks. At a time when Turkey's ethnically diverse
society is increasingly divided over Islamist and secular lines, Erdoğan is unable to

[27] Fighters on Syrian-Turkish border may be Qaeda allies: Russia, Reuters, July 25, 2012
[28] Turkey opts for SCO, The Voice of Russia, July 27, 2012
[29] Turkey's Hatay Province, Mossad, CIA spy hub: Turkish MP, PressTV, July 31, 2012

persuade the majority opinion to support a war in Syria, something which would cost the Turkish state immensely. While being in close contact with Washington and Tel Aviv to discuss "a broad range of contingency plans" over "how to manage a Syrian government collapse," Ankara has hosted and financially supported the Syrian National Council, the Free Syrian Army, the Syrian Muslim Brotherhood, and has shown itself to be fully committed to toppling the Syrian government. Since severely straining relations after a May 2010 incident involving the slaying of nine Turks by Israeli commandos who tried to stop a Turkish ship from breaking the Gaza blockade, Tel Aviv and Ankara have converged once more to cooperate against the Assad government:

A normalized Turkish-Israeli relationship would also open opportunities for cooperation against the Assad government, with the Turks taking the political and regional lead and the Israelis providing intelligence and additional practical assets. Any Israeli contribution would, of course, have to be invisible in order not to create a sense that Israel was behind the Syrian uprising. This makes Turkish-Israeli cooperation against Mr. Assad even more valuable, for it would allow Israel to provide untraceable assets to support Turkey's efforts to undermine the Assad government. [30]

Israel's Mossad has quietly directed support to Salafist fighters and armed rebel groups from the onset of the uprising in southern Syria in March 2011. Additionally, they have also provided support to Kurdish separatists in northern Syria allied with Massoud Barzani's Kurdish Regional Government in Iraq.[31] Kurdish separatism is the vehicle of choice for foreign powers to weaken Syria's territorial integrity by balkanization along ethnic and religious lines in order to form acquiescent political entities. For Tel Aviv, this strategy is fundamental to Israeli expansionism and serves to isolate their larger adversary in Tehran.

Israel and the Path to Persia

Since the 1967 Six Day War, Israel has illegally occupied an area of southwestern Syria, known as the Golan Heights, a region that Tel Aviv relies on for one-third of its fresh water supplies.[32] Historically, Israel has shown interest in exploring the Golan Heights' petroleum and natural gas reserves – initiatives that were suspended under previous administrations' peace negotiations with Syria. In an attempt to decrease Tel Aviv's reliance on oil exports, Israeli Prime Minister Benjamin Netanyahu's government has taken advantage of civil unrest in Syria to approve exploratory drilling in the Golan Heights, a move likely to trigger international uproar and potential conflict between Israel's Arab neighbors if energy resources are indeed found.[33] While fanning the flames of insurgency inside Syria, Netanyahu and Israeli Defense Minister Ehud Barak assert that Tel Aviv would be prepared to attack Syria with the aim of targeting its weapons arsenals should the situation deteriorate.[34] While Netanyahu publically announced support for a Palestinian state on the West

---

[30] How America Can Help Its Friends Make Nice, The New York Times, June 20, 2012
[31] Veteran Kurdish politician calls on Israel to support the break-up of Syria, Kurd Net, May 16, 2012
[32] Shouting in the hills, Al-Ahram, June 2008
[33] Government secretly approves Golan Heights drilling, The Times of Israel, May 13, 2012
[34] Netanyahu 'determined to attack Iran' before US elections, claims Israel's Channel 10, The Times of Israel, August 20, 2012

Bank, a panel of Israeli jurists assembled by Netanyahu's government to determine the legal status of the West Bank concluded that there is "no occupation" of Palestinian lands and that the continued construction of settlement outposts are entirely legal under Israeli law, regardless of international opinion. Netanyahu's administration has approved construction of 850 settler homes in the occupied West Bank in June 2012, even after the Israeli parliament rejected a bill to retroactively legalize some of the existing homes in the area.[35] While Israel's Foreign Minister Avigdor Lieberman asserts Tel Aviv's unwillingness to permit Palestinians any right to return to their lands, emphasizing, "not even one refugee," apartheid enforced on ethnic and religious lines has become a ratified part of Israeli government policy.[36]

In 1952, Israeli Defense Minister Moshe Dayan spoke ardently of Tel Aviv's ultimate goal, the creation of "an Israeli empire." Netanyahu's conservative Likud party was founded on the ideological foundations of Revisionist Zionism, promoting Jewish settlement in Judea and Samaria (the West Bank) and the full biblical land of Israel by contemporary Jews, an oil-rich landmass extending from the banks of the Nile River in Egypt to the shores of the Euphrates. The Movement for Greater Israel was founded following the capture of the West Bank and Gaza Strip from Jordan and Egypt during 1967's Six Day War, leading to the wider construction of Israeli settlements. Israel's Likud party was established on the philosophy of Ze'ev Jabotinksy, who called for the establishment of a "Greater Israel," a concept embraced by Israeli historian Benzion Netanyahu, father of the Israel's Prime Minister who was quoted in an interview before his death in 2012 as saying:

"The Bible finds no worse image than this of the man from the desert. And why? Because he has no respect for any law. Because in the desert he can do as he pleases," Benzion Netanyahu said. "The tendency towards conflict is in the essence of the Arab. He is an enemy by essence. His personality won't allow him any compromise or agreement. It doesn't matter what kind of resistance he will meet, what price he will pay. His existence is one of perpetual war." Israel's must be the same, he indicated. "The two states solution doesn't exist," Benzion Netanyahu said. "There are no two people here. There is a Jewish people and an Arab population... there is no Palestinian people, so you don't create a state for an imaginary nation... they only call themselves a people in order to fight the Jews." [37]

While openly advocating programs of such substantial territorial expansion have fallen out of mainstream Israeli policy goals, adherents to hyper-conservative Zionism view Israeli expansionism as the unwavering obligation of the Jewish people. Undoubtedly, the country that most challenges these ambitions is the Islamic Republic of Iran. Although nuclear-armed Israel presides over perhaps the most capable army in the Middle East and is nowhere near as vulnerable as Europe's Jewish population prior to World War II (Netanyahu often contrasts the Holocaust with the impending threat posed by Iran), Netanyahu's administration has asserted

---

[35] Israel to build more West Bank homes, Al-Jazeera, June 07, 2012

[36] Lieberman: Netanyahu's stance on 1967 borders reflects viewpoint of most Israelis, The Times of Israel, May 23, 2011

[37] Received Wisdom? How the Ideology of Netanyahu's Late Father Influenced the Son, TIME, May 02, 2012

its right to strike Iran without consent from any other nation in order to prevent Tehran from developing the capability to produce nuclear weapons.[38]

Senior officials within Israel have been vocal in their criticisms of the Netanyahu government's defense policies, such as IDF Chief of Staff Lt. Gen. Benny Gantz, who advised against attacking Syrian chemical weapon convoys, advising further caution and restraint.[39] Former Mossad chief Meir Dagan has been a vocal critic against the Netanyahu government's plans to attack Iran, calling it, "the stupidest thing I have ever heard," warning of wider regional war.[40] Netanyahu has insinuated that non-terrestrial matters guide Tehran's foreign policy, being critical of Shi'a religious beliefs practiced in Iran, which prophesize the return of a direct descendent of the founder of Islam, Al-Imam al-Mahdi, during times of turmoil and decadence to bring order through the authentic interpretation of Islam, despite himself being widely criticized for espousing a megalomaniacal hubris, and emphasizing a messianic-catastrophic worldview, where Israel is "the eternal nation." [41]

In an interview with 60 Minutes, Meir Dagan emphasized the rationality of the Iranian regime, while former Shin Bet security service chief Yuval Diskin has publicly rejected calls to militarily strike Iran, accusing Tel Aviv of exacerbating the situation.[42] While these senior Israeli officials fear the possible ramifications of a direct strike on Iran, most advocate regime change in Tehran. Former Mossad chief Ephraim Halevy argues that talk of Iran posing an "existential threat" to Israel is merely Tel Aviv attempting to garner support of the international community by making insinuations to the historical plight of Jews.[43] Halevy has emphasized that Iran and Israel should formally make agreements that Tehran will not to weaponize its nuclear energy program, allowing Iran to be "reintroduced into the family of nations from which they have been virtually expelled in recent months." International sanctions and oil embargoes on Iran have caused inflation to soar, with the cost of food in Iran increasing between 25 and125 percent, with 60 percent of the population relying on cash subsidies handed out by Tehran.[44] As the Iranian rial continues to plunge while commodity prices continue to skyrocket, former Israeli foreign minister Shlomo Ben-Ami forewarns, "When a national currency loses 50% of its value in a matter of weeks, economic collapse is at hand." [45] *Haaretz* reports the remarks of an unnamed senior official in the Israeli Foreign Ministry:

These aren't sanctions against Iran. Instead, they are sanctions imposed by the West to curb Israel's attack plans. Had Israel not spoken out about its intention to attack, none of this would be happening. The Iranians are frightened. You have to understand

---

[38] Bad news unwelcome: Israel refuses to listen to US envoy's report on Iran, Russia Today, May 26, 2012

[39] Attack on Syrian chemical stockpiles could lead to 'broader campaign,' says IDF Chief of Staff, Haaretz, July 24, 2012

[40] Ex-Mossad boss Meir Dagan says an Israeli attack on Iran would be 'stupidest thing ever,' The New York Times, March 11, 2012

[41] As Netanyahu pushes Israel closer to war with Iran, Israelis cannot keep silent, Haaretz, August 03, 2012

[42] Yuval Diskin, Israel Former Intel Chief, Slams Netanyahu's Iran Stance, The Huffington Post, April 28, 2012

[43] Iran poses no 'existential threat' to Israel - ex-Mossad chief, Russia Today, February 06, 2012

[44] No One Can Afford Another Round of Iran Sanctions, OilPrice, May 21, 2012

[45] Iran's Nuclear Grass Eaters, Project Syndicate, April 04, 2012

what's going on there in stores; citizens grab food off the shelves because they are worried about an impending attack. Inflation is soaring and the currency has lost half its value. All this attests to fear. [46]

While Iranian Foreign Minister Ali Akbar Salehi publically renounces the development of nuclear weapons, Iranian scientists claim to be enriching uranium to 20% to develop radiopharmaceuticals and industrial isotopes under the supervision of inspectors of the International Atomic Energy Agency (IAEA).[47] Iran has made efforts to ensure the transparency of its nuclear program by allowing IAEA probes to inspect Iranian sites such as the Fordo enrichment plant and Parchin military complex, where the agency has reported suspicious activities in the past. Former chief of the International Atomic Energy Agency (IAEA) Hans Blix has challenged the IAEA's own reports on Iran's nuclear activities, accusing the agency of relying on unverified intelligence from the US and Israel.[48] The IAEA's May 2012 report cited Tehran's progress toward enrichment technology with complete cooperation with the agency, confirming the non-weaponized status of Iranian nuclear activities.[49] Clinton Bastin, former director of US nuclear weapons production programs, has sent an open letter to President Obama in December 2011 regarding the status of Iran's capacity to produce nuclear weapons. Bastin reiterates:

The ultimate product of Iran's gas centrifuge facilities would be highly enriched uranium hexafluoride, a gas that cannot be used to make a weapon. Converting the gas to metal, fabricating components and assembling them with high explosives using dangerous and difficult technology that has never been used in Iran would take many years after a diversion of three tons of low enriched uranium gas from fully safeguarded inventories. The resulting weapon, if intended for delivery by missile, would have a yield equivalent to that of a kiloton of conventional high explosives. [50]

Bastin's assessment of Iran's nuclear program further emphasizes the impracticality of weaponizing the hexafluoride product of Tehran's gas-centrifuges, as it would produce a highly inefficient nuclear weapon. If Iran chose to produce nuclear weapons in this way, it would take several years to reach the 90% enrichment levels needed for a nuclear deterrent. In March 2012, Reuters released a special report entitled, "Intel shows Iran nuclear threat not imminent", concluding that the United States, its European allies and even Israel agree that Tehran does not have a bomb, it has not decided to build one, and it is years away from having a deliverable nuclear warhead.[51] Despite evidence that Iran does not possess the capability to build nuclear weapons, and with no indication of Tehran attempting to do so, leaders in Tel Aviv have asserted their right to conduct military strikes against Iran before the US Presidential elections in November 2012.[52] Following a terrorist

---

[46] Israeli threats of attack sparked new wave of Iran sanctions, officials say, Israel, May 16, 2012

[47] Iranian Experts Place Fuel Plates into Heart of Tehran Research Reactor, FARS, May 23, 2012

[48] Blix: US, Israel source most of IAEA allegations, PressTV, May 25, 2012

[49] Envoy: UN Atomic Report Endorses Peaceful Nature of Iran's N. Activities, FARS, May 05, 2012

[50] Top US Nuclear Expert Tells Obama: There Is No Weapons Threat From Iran, LarouchePac, February 25, 2012

[51] SPECIAL REPORT-Intel shows Iran nuclear threat not imminent, Reuters, March 23, 2012

[52] Israel takes back promise to Obama not to attack Iran before the election, Russia Today, May 24, 2012

attack targeting a bus in Bulgaria that killed five Israeli tourists in July 2012, Netanyahu immediately issued statements accusing Hezbollah and Iran of being responsible for the attacks, stating:

Iran must be exposed by the international community as the premier terrorist support state that it is, and everything should be done to prevent Iran, the world's most dangerous regime, from developing the world's most dangerous weapons. [53]

The possibility of Israel directly striking chemical weapons convoys in Syria and infiltrating its territory, or striking Iran's nuclear energy sites, will yield dangerous consequences for the entire region, and the global economy. Contrary to claims of institutional anti-Semitism emanating from Tehran, the founder of the Islamic Republic, Ayatollah Ruhollah Khomeini, referred to Judaism as an honored branch of the same tree of monotheism that produced Islam (the largest population of Jews in the Middle East outside of Israel reside in Iran), while state media has distinguished between Jews and Zionists, the latter being viewed as the movement to forcefully claim Jewish territorial hegemony in what they regard as the heart of the Muslim world.[54] While behind closed doors US policy makers admit Iran, even if it were to obtain nuclear weapons, is driven by self-preservation and protecting the influence it is steadily gaining throughout the Middle Eastern region it borders, the message they desperately seek to relate to the public is one of an irrational, apocalyptic theocracy eager to usher in Armageddon. Reports issued by the RAND corporation note that Iran has had chemical weapons in its inventory for decades, describing the strict control that military units exercise over these weapons, making it unlikely they would end up in the hands of "terrorists," or even Hezbollah.[55] The fact that Iran's extensive chemical weapon stockpile has yet to be dispersed into the hands of non-state actors, along with the fact that these same military units would in turn handle any Iranian nuclear weapons, lends further evidence to the conclusion that Iran is indeed driven by self-preservation and self-defense.

While the argument ensues over whether or not Iran should have nuclear weapons or if it intends to commit genocide against the Jews, the war against Tehran has been meticulously planned in advanced and has already quietly begun. The Brookings Institution, a US-based think-tank, was founded on grants given by the Carnegie Corporation, the Rockefeller Foundation and the Ford Foundation, and receives funding from corporate sponsors such as Bank of America, Goldman Sachs, Lockheed Martin, Exxon, Boeing, General Electric, and others. In 2009, the Brooking Institute issued a lengthy report titled, "Which Path to Persia?" examining ways in which the United States can influence regime change in Tehran.[56] The opening pages of the report cite acknowledgments given by the Smith Richardson Foundation, upon which US foreign policy theoretician Zbigniew Brzezinski sits as an acting governor. The sheer scale of the military options considered by Brookings' strategy would create immense profits for the defense contractors that sponsor it, regardless of the operation's success. The report opens with the frank declaration that Iran is a

---

[53] Benjamin Netanyahu: Iran is the most dangerous regime in the world, The Telegraph, July 19, 2012

[54] Iran's Jews reject cash offer to move to Israel, The Guardian, July 12, 2007

[55] Integrating Counterproliferation into Defense Planning, RAND Corporation, 2007

[56] Which Path to Persia? The Brookings Institution, June 2009

confounding nation that undermines America's interests and influence in the Middle East. Not once is it mentioned that the Islamic Republic poses any direct threat to the security of the United States itself. In fact, Iran is described as a nation intentionally avoiding provocations that would justify military operations to be conducted against it. Iran's motivations are listed as being ideological, nationalistic, and security driven - very understandable, considering the condition of its neighbors, who have been invaded and occupied by foreign forces. The crux of the issue is that America's interests in the region, not security, motivate it to confront Iran, a theme that repeats itself incessantly throughout the 156-page report.

• **Sanctions (Page 39)**

For those who favor regime change or a military attack on Iran (either by the United States or Israel), there is a strong argument to be made for trying this option first. Inciting regime change in Iran would be greatly assisted by convincing the Iranian people that their government is so ideologically blinkered that it refuses to do what is best for the people and instead clings to a policy that could only bring ruin on the country. The ideal scenario in this case would be that the United States and the international community present a package of positive inducements so enticing that the Iranian citizenry would support the deal, only to have the regime reject it.

In a similar vein, any military operation against Iran will likely be very unpopular around the world and require the proper international context—both to ensure the logistical support the operation would require and to minimize the blowback from it. The best way to minimize international opprobrium and maximize support (however grudging or covert), is to strike only when there is a widespread conviction that the Iranians were given but then rejected a superb offer—one so good that only a regime determined to acquire nuclear weapons and acquire them for the wrong reasons would turn it down. Under those circumstances, the United States (or Israel) could portray its operations as taken in sorrow, not anger, and at least some in the international community would conclude that the Iranians "brought it on themselves" by refusing a very good deal.

Regime change and perhaps even military operations against Iran are talked about as a foregone conclusion, with the Brookings Institution using the pretext of sanctions as merely a means of incremental escalation to tip-toe the world into backing regime change, including war if need be. Brookings suggests coercing the Iranian government, without regime change, through crippling sanctions versus incentives. The proposed incentives, in turn, appear more a relief from American imposed economic punishment than anything of actual substance. Brookings suggests "security guarantees" from an American invasion to address the very real concerns that would motivate Iran to construct nuclear weapons in the first place, noting that concrete action would be needed by the US in order to fulfill this incentive, including drawing down US forces in the Middle East, a concession Brookings itself admits is highly unlikely over the next several decades.

Brookings interjects at this point, a brazen admission that under no circumstance should the US grant Iran a position of dominance, nor should there be any ambiguity about what Washington sees as Tehran's role in the region. This option of "persuasion" appears to have already played out and failed, both in drawing concessions from Iran through meaningless offers and at marshaling the international support needed to make additional sanctions effective. Brookings's report notes on Page 24, that the real threat is not the deployment of nuclear weapons, but rather the deterrence they present, allowing Iran to counter US influence in the region without the fear of an American invasion. In other words, the playing field would become level and America may be forced to recognize Iran's national sovereignty in regards to its own regional interests. The report concedes that Iran's leadership may be aggressive, but not reckless. The possession of nuclear weapons would be used as an absolute last resort, considering American and even Israeli nuclear deterrence capabilities.

• Invasion (Page 65)

If the United States were to decide that, to garner greater international support, galvanize U.S. domestic support, and/or provide a legal justification for an invasion, it would be best to wait for an Iranian provocation, then the time frame for an invasion might stretch out indefinitely. With only one real exception, since the 1979 revolution, the Islamic Republic has never willingly provoked an American military response, although it certainly has taken actions that could have done so if Washington had been looking for a fight.

Thus it is not impossible that Tehran might take some action that would justify an American invasion and it is certainly the case that if Washington sought such a provocation, it could take actions that might make it more likely that Tehran would do so (although being too obvious about this could nullify the provocation). However, since it would be up to Iran to make the provocative move, which Iran has been wary of doing most times in the past, the United States would never know for sure when it would get the requisite Iranian provocation. In fact, it might never come at all.

This excerpt is nothing less than US policy-makers openly talking about purposefully provoking a nation in order to justify a full-scale invasion that would otherwise be untenable. If such treachery, at the cost of thousands of American lives and perhaps millions of Iranian lives, is openly talked about within the halls of these corporate-funded think tanks, what do they talk about that isn't on record? Indeed, a conventional war with Iran is currently impossible, as acknowledged by the Brookings Institution. What is worrying is that they believe it would not be impossible if only America were presented with the "proper" provocations. Brookings's experts go on to say that Washington could take "certain actions" to ensure such provocations took place.

Furthermore, Brookings states that Iran has already gone through extreme measures specifically not to react to American provocations, raising the specter that provocations may take the shape of a staged event instead, should full-scale invasion be sought.

• United Front Against Iran (Page 66)

Most European, Asian, and Middle Eastern publics are dead set against any American military action against Iran derived from the current differences between Iran and the international community—let alone Iran and the United States. Other than a Tehran-sponsored 9/11, it is hard to imagine what would change their minds.

For many democracies and some fragile autocracies to which Washington would be looking for support, this public antipathy is likely to prove decisive. For instance, Saudi Arabia is positively apoplectic about the Iranians' nuclear program, as well as about their mischief-making in Lebanon, Iraq, and the Palestinian territories. Yet, so far, Riyadh has made clear that it will not support military operations of any kind against Iran. Certainly that could change, but it is hard to imagine what it would take.

Given that this situation has not been enough to push the GCC to support military operations against Iran, what would? Certainly, Iran testing a nuclear device might, but at that point, it almost certainly would be too late: if the United States is going to invade Iran, it will want to do so before Iran has developed actual nuclear weapons, not after. It is hard to know what else Iran could do that would change GCC attitudes about the use of force unless new leaders took power in the Gulf who were far more determined to stop Iran than the current leadership is.

As the excerpt makes mention of "new leaders" taking over in the Gulf, funding and support for insurgents in Syria by US allies such as Saudi Arabia indicates that the Kingdom's foreign policy and that of the Gulf Cooperation Council is in line with Washington and Tel Aviv's objectives in the region. Undoubtedly, leaders of nations in the Persian Gulf would favor bringing about destabilization covertly, through the kind of insurgency and psychological operations carried out in Syria, rather than open military confrontation or strikes led by Washington or Tel Aviv.

• Manufacturing Provocations (Page 84 - 85)

It would be far more preferable if the United States could cite an Iranian provocation as justification for the airstrikes before launching them. Clearly, the more outrageous, the more deadly, and the more unprovoked the Iranian action, the better off the United States would be. Of course, it would be very difficult for the United States to goad Iran into such a provocation without the rest of the world recognizing this game, which would then undermine it. (One method that would have some possibility of success would be to ratchet up covert regime change efforts in the hope that Tehran would retaliate overtly, or even semi-overtly, which could then be portrayed as an unprovoked act of Iranian aggression.)

This suggests that this option might benefit from being held in abeyance until such time as the Iranians made an appropriately provocative move, as they do from time to time. In that case, it would be less a determined policy to employ airstrikes and, instead, more of an opportunistic hope that Iran would provide the United States with the kind of provocation that would justify airstrikes. However, that would mean that the use of airstrikes could not be the primary U.S. policy toward Iran (even if it were Washington's fervent preference), but merely an ancillary contingency to another option that would be the primary policy unless and until Iran provided the necessary pretext.

The plotting of a deceitful gambit to goad a sovereign nation into war is again in sight, a notion Brookings notes time and time again since Iran has no interest in armed conflict with the United States. The reference to "covert regime change efforts" is used as a means of applying pressure to further political escalation and subsequent military intervention. Such strategies describe the kind of violent scenarios that have unfolded in Libya and Syria, where foreign support encouraged the use of violence, to which national governments were forced to react, with the response then serving as an impetus for expanded foreign intervention. Brookings notes that such provocations must be carried out without raising suspicions of the "game" being played throughout the world, insinuating the loss of credibility that would come with mainstream acknowledgement of long institutionalized aggression and foreign subversion.

• Foreign-Funded Color Revolution (Page 105)

The United States could play multiple roles in facilitating a revolution. By funding and helping organize domestic rivals of the regime, the United States could create an alternative leadership to seize power. As Raymond Tanter of the Iran Policy Committee argues, students and other groups "need covert backing for their demonstrations. They need fax machines. They need internet access, funds to duplicate materials, and funds to keep vigilantes from beating them up." Beyond this, U.S.-backed media outlets could highlight regime shortcomings and make otherwise obscure critics more prominent. The United States already supports Persian-language satellite television (Voice of America Persian) and radio (Radio Farda) that bring unfiltered news to Iranians (in recent years, these have taken the lion's share of overt U.S. funding for promoting democracy in Iran). U.S. economic pressure (and perhaps military pressure as well) can discredit the regime, making the population hungry for a rival leadership.

Policy-makers at the Brookings Institution make outright calls to create the conditions within Iran, or any target nation for that matter, that are likely to coax civil unrest. They suggest funding and organizing that unrest and using domestic and foreign media to manipulate public perception and perpetuate US-backed anti-Tehran propaganda. This model is used in nearly every country targeted for destabilization, generally funded by organizations like the National Endowment for Democracy (NED), so-called "independent media" organizations and human rights NGOs that "make otherwise obscure critics more prominent." The NED-funded Project on Middle East Democracy is one such propaganda outlet operating throughout the Middle East, propagating the official US narrative in regards to unrest fomented from Egypt to Syria. Brookings openly mentions *Voice of America*'s Farsi language service, while other examples include Southeast Asia's NED-funded Prachatai of Thailand, and Radio Free Europe in Eastern Europe, a subsidiary with VOA under the Broadcasting Board of Governors, upon which Secretary of State Hillary Clinton sits as a member. This global network of "democracy promotion" feeds the mainstream media their talking points, which are then repeated verbatim or cited outright as reputable sources. Brookings's admission that these institutions exist to protect and expand US interests throughout the region, while diminishing Iran's ability to challenge those interests, is significant. This admission demonstrates conclusively that these various institutions do not serve to promote democracy, protect freedom, or even protect America from a genuine security threat, but rather serve the geopolitical and strategic objectives of the United States.

• Assisting Popular Revolutions with Military Force (Page 109 - 110)

Consequently, if the United States ever succeeds in sparking a revolt against the clerical regime, Washington may have to consider whether to provide it [the revolt] with some form of military support to prevent Tehran from crushing it. This requirement means that a popular revolution in Iran does not seem to fit the model of the "velvet revolutions" that occurred elsewhere. The point is that the Iranian regime may not be willing to go gently into that good night; instead, and unlike so many Eastern European regimes, it may choose to fight to the death. In those circumstances, if there is not external military assistance to the revolutionaries, they might not just fail but be massacred. Consequently, if the United States is to pursue this policy, Washington must take this possibility into consideration. It adds some very important requirements to the list: either the policy must include ways to weaken the Iranian military or weaken the willingness of the regime's leaders to call on the military, or else the United States must be ready to intervene to defeat it.

Quite clearly, after previously conspiring to implement foreign-funded unrest, the predictable crackdown by Iranian security forces to restore order "requires" some form of deterrent or military support to be employed in order to prevent the movement from being crushed. This scenario materialized in Libya, where foreign-funded insurgents were likened to "unarmed civilians" shortly after their rebellion began, prior to NATO forces intervening to prevent the armed uprising from being defeated by Gaddafi's forces.

• US Sponsored Terrorism (Page 113)

The United States could work with groups like the Iraq-based National Council of Resistance of Iran (NCRI) and its military wing, the Mujahedin-e Khalq (MEK), helping the thousands of its members who, under Saddam Husayn's regime, were armed and had conducted guerrilla and terrorist operations against the clerical regime. Although the NCRI is supposedly disarmed today, that could quickly be changed.

• Mujahedin-e Khalq & Armed Insurgency (Page 117 – 118 & 121)

Perhaps the most prominent (and certainly the most controversial) opposition group that has attracted attention as a potential U.S. proxy is the NCRI (National Council of Resistance of Iran), the political movement established by the MEK (Mujahedin-e Khalq). Critics believe the group to be undemocratic and unpopular, and indeed anti-American. In contrast, the group's champions contend that the movement's long-standing opposition to the Iranian regime and record of successful attacks on and intelligence-gathering operations against the regime make it worthy of U.S. support. They also argue that the group is no longer anti-American and question the merit of earlier accusations. Raymond Tanter, one of the group's supporters in the United States, contends that the MEK and the NCRI are allies for regime change in Tehran and also act as a useful proxy for gathering intelligence. The MEK's greatest intelligence coup was the provision of intelligence in 2002 that led to the discovery of a secret site in Iran for enriching uranium.

Despite its defenders' claims, the MEK remains on the U.S. government list of foreign terrorist organizations. In the 1970s, the group killed three U.S. officers and three civilian contractors in Iran. During the 1979-1980 hostage crisis, the group praised the decision to take American hostages and Elaine Sciolino reported that, while group leaders publicly condemned the 9/11 attacks, within the group celebrations were widespread. Undeniably, the group has conducted terrorist attacks—often excused by the MEK's advocates because they are directed against the Iranian government. For example, in 1981, the group bombed the headquarters of the Islamic Republic Party, which was then the clerical leadership's main political organization, killing an estimated 70 senior officials. More recently, the group has claimed credit for over a dozen mortar attacks, assassinations, and other assaults on Iranian civilian and military targets between 1998 and 2001. At the very least, to work more closely with the group (at least in an overt manner), Washington would need to remove it from the list of foreign terrorist organizations.

An articled published in the *New Yorker* by journalist Seymour Hersh titled, "Our Men in Iran?" documents how members of Mujahideen-e-Khalq (MEK), an Iranian dissident group and US State Department-listed terrorist organization, were trained in communications, cryptography, small-unit tactics and weaponry by the Joint Special Operations Command (JSOC) at a base in Nevada starting in 2005.[57] JSOC instructed MEK operatives on how to penetrate major Iranian communications systems, allowing the group to intercept telephone calls and text messages inside Iran for the purpose of sharing them with American intelligence. The group has been implicated in the assassination of Iranian nuclear scientists and the planting of the Stuxnet malware that sabotaged Iran's nuclear facility in Natanz. [58]

MEK was founded in 1965 as a Marxist Islamic mass political movement aimed at agitating the monarchy of the US-backed Iranian Shah, Mohammad Reza Pahlavi. The group initially sided with revolutionary clerics led by Ayatollah Khomeini following the 1979 Islamic Revolution, but eventually turned away from the regime during a power struggle that resulted in the group waging urban guerilla warfare against Iran's Revolutionary Guards in 1981. The organization was later given refuge by Saddam Hussein and mounted attacks on Iran from within Iraqi territory, killing an estimated 17,000 Iranian nationals in the process.[59] MEK exists as the main component of the Paris-based National Council of Resistance of Iran (NCRI), a "coalition of democratic Iranian organizations, groups and personalities," calling itself a "parliament-in-exile" and seeking to "establish a democratic, secular and coalition government" in Iran. Following the toppling of Saddam Hussein, UN special representative in Iraq Martin Kobler organized efforts to relocate MEK insurgents to a former US military base near the Baghdad airport, with the full support of the US Embassy in Iraq and the State Department in order to avoid violent clashes between the MEK and the Shiite-led Iraqi government.[60]

MEK has long received material assistance from Israel, who assisted the organization with broadcasting into Iran from their political base in Paris, while the MEK and NCRI have reportedly provided the United States with intelligence on Iran's nuclear program. Despite the documented cases of atrocities committed by MEK forces, elder statesmen such as former NATO Supreme Allied Commander General Wesley K. Clark, former New York City Mayor Rudy Giuliani, and former 9/11 Commission Chairman Lee Hamilton were paid $20,000 to $30,000 per engagement

57 Our Men in Iran? The New Yorker, April 06, 2012
58 Israel teams with terror group to kill Iran's nuclear scientists, U.S. officials tell NBC News, NBC, February 09, 2012
59 Moqtada Sadr Reiterates Iraqis' Demand for Expulsion of MKO Terrorists, FARS, September 09, 2011
60 Are the MEK's U.S. friends its worst enemies? Foreign Policy, March 08, 2012

to endorse the removal of the Mujahideen-e Khalq from the US State Department's list of Foreign Terrorist Organizations.[61] A recent investigation by the US Treasury Department has indicated that the Mujahedin-e Khalq Organization is financially sponsored by the Israeli regime and Saudi Arabia.[62] Upon launching a war against Iran, aggressor nations would likely utilize MEK forces as opposition insurgents and could even recognize the touted "parliament-in-exile", the National Council of Resistance of Iran, as Iran's "legitimate representative," much like the Friends of Syria group has recognized the opposition Syrian National Council.[63]

• Potential Ethnic Proxies (Page 113)

For instance, the United States could opt to work primarily with various unhappy Iranian ethnic groups (Kurds, Baloch, Arabs, and so on) who have fought the regime at various periods since the revolution. A coalition of ethnic opposition movements, particularly if combined with dissident Persians, would pose a serious threat to regime stability. In addition, the unrest the groups themselves create could weaken the regime at home. At the least, the regime would have to divert resources to putting down the rebellions. At most, the unrest might discredit the regime overtime, weakening its position vis-à-vis its rivals.

Despite the shameless bravado displayed throughout the entire report, no section is as unsettling as the one titled "Inspiring an Insurgency," where Brookings outright advocates the funding, training, and triggering of a full-blown armed insurgency against the government of Iran. The report specifically mentions Ahvazi Arab separatists, who would later be the subject of Seymour Hersh's "Preparing the Battlefield" where he exposes the option as already being set in motion within Iran.[64] Ethnic Kurds in the North, and Baloch rebels near Pakistan in the East are also mentioned as potential recipients of US aid in conducting their campaigns of armed terror against the Iranian people. The CIA is selected to handle supplies and training, while Brookings suggests that options for more direct military support also be considered. In their subsection, "Finding a Proxy," Brookings describes how the use of ethnic tensions could fuel unrest. It laments the fact that many ethnic minorities still hold nationalism as a priority along with their fellow Persians. Despite being on America's official terrorist list for having previously killed US military men, the Mujahedin-e Khalq are given ample consideration within Brookings's report. In their subsection, "Finding a Conduit and Safe Haven," Brookings describes various methods of harboring their stable of US-funded terrorists within the nations currently occupied by US troops and how to ferry them in and out of Iran between operations. Certainly, if the United States went through with arming and funding MEK, they themselves would become "state sponsors of terrorism" - even as they continue to fight a decade-long war against supposedly just that. MEK is unequivocally a terrorist organization that indiscriminately targets civilians along with their political opponents, and yet, they are considered a potential proxy, and considerations for their removal from the apparently meaningless "foreign terrorist

---

[61] Mujahideen-e Khalq: Former U.S. Officials Make Millions Advocating For Terrorist Organization, The Huffington Post, July 08, 2012
[62] Israel funds terrorist MKO: Investigation, PressTV, May 24, 2012
[63] Friends of Syria recognize SNC as 'legitimate representative,' Russia Today, April 01, 2012
[64] Preparing the Battlefield, The New Yorker, July 07, 2007

organizations" list are based solely on their usefulness in advancing US foreign policy.

• Fomenting a Military Coup (Page 123 - 124)

Mounting a coup is hard work, especially in a state as paranoid about foreign influence and meddling as Iran is. The United States would first have to make contact with members of Iran's military (and likely its security services as well). This by itself is very difficult. Because of Iranian hypersensitivity to Americans, the United States would likely have to rely on "cutouts"—third party nationals working on behalf of the United States—which invariably introduces considerable complexity. Then the United States would have to use those contacts to try to identify Iranian military personnel who were both willing and able to stage a coup, which would be more difficult still; it would be hard enough for Americans to make contact with Iranian military officers, let alone make contact with those specific individuals willing to risk their lives and their families in a coup attempt.

Of course, it is possible that if Washington makes very clear that it is trying to support a coup in Iran, the coup plotters will reach out to the United States. But this is very rare: history shows that coup plotters willing to expose themselves to another national government are usually discovered and killed; furthermore, most of those coming to the United States to ask for help overthrowing this or that government tend to be poseurs or even counterintelligence agents of the targeted government.

It should be noted that the Brookings report suggests that all options - popular revolution, insurgency, and coup - be used concurrently in the hopes that at least one may succeed. It also suggests that "helpful synergies" might be created among them to further mire the targeted regime. The Brookings report itself makes reference to the historical precedence of the United States successfully "mounting a coup" in Iran, providing 1953's Operation Ajax as a notable example:

Although many coups are homegrown, one obvious historic model of a foreign-assisted coup in Iran is Operation Ajax, the 1953 coup d'état that overthrew the government of Prime Minister Mohammed Mossadeq and reinstated the rule of Shah Reza Pahlavi. To carry out the coup, the CIA and British intelligence supported General Fazlollah Zahedi, providing him and his followers with money and propaganda, as well as helping organize their activities. (Page 150)

It is inconceivable that one could read the pages of "Which Path to Persia?" and not understand the current "international community" as anything less than absolutely illegitimate. Western leaders have historically contrived a myriad of laws with which to restrain and eliminate their competition, while remaining entirely uninhibited themselves in their own overt criminality, extorting and coercing the world to conform to its "interests." This report represents the full array of options not only for use in Iran, but throughout the world. With the US-funded "Arab Spring" as a real world model, one can plainly see how the methodology outlined in the report has been used to destabilize and depose regimes as well as instigate wars of aggression. It is essential that reports of this nature be widely circulated and made public knowledge, exposing the methodology and architects of aggressive Western foreign policy. As the report itself states numerous times, the vast majority of their gambits require secrecy, "plausible deniability," to carry out their ideas "without the rest of the world recognizing this game."

Despite the shortcomings of the administration in Tehran, lawmakers and senior officials have advocated international cooperation, dialogue and pragmatism with regard to the Syrian issue. On August 9th, 2012, Iran hosted an International Consultative Conference, bringing together representatives of thirty nations to call for ending the flow of foreign arms into terrorist hands inside Syria, proposals to broker a meaningful ceasefire, the coordination of humanitarian aid, and support for Syrian people's right to reform without foreign interference.[65] The unique conference featured representatives of over half of the world's population, including nations such as Russia, China, India, Pakistan, Indonesia, and Venezuela, signaling that, indeed, Syria's government is not as "isolated" as portrayed by Western media. The United States downplayed the significance of the conference and criticized the Islamic Republic for supporting Bashar al-Assad's government. Iran's stance on Syria is best elaborated in an August 2012 Op-Ed in the Washington Post, authored by Iranian Foreign Minister Ali Akbar Salehi:

Iran seeks a solution that is in the interest of everyone. Syrian society is a beautiful mosaic of ethnicities, faiths and cultures, and it will be smashed to pieces should President Bashar al-Assad abruptly fall. The idea that, in that event, there would be an orderly transition of power is an illusion. Abrupt political change without a roadmap for managed political transition will lead only to a precarious situation that would destabilize one of the world's most sensitive regions. Iran is part of the solution, not the problem. As the world has witnessed during the past decade, we have acted as a stabilizing force in Iraq and Afghanistan, two other Muslim countries thrown into turmoil. The stability of our region is paramount for world peace and tranquility. [66]

Tehran has supported Kofi Annan's six-point plan and has shown willingness to facilitate talks between the Syrian government and the opposition. Foreign Minister Salehi has reiterated Tehran's support for the kind of political reform that will ensure that people have the right to participate in free and fair presidential elections under international supervision. Furthermore, Iran has opposed "any foreign interference and military intervention in resolving the Syrian crisis" and has provided medical and humanitarian aid to Syria through the Iranian Red Crescent.[67] Undoubtedly, Iran's efforts at diplomatically negotiating an end to the Syrian conflict deserve respect and appropriate acknowledgement. The rationality of Tehran's approach is ultimately a testament to Iran's value as a responsible and viable member of the international community.

The Sino-Russian Position

While the Syrian conflict has deeply divided international opinion, the steady non-interventionist stance of Russia and China has been subjected to harsh criticism for preventing the United Nations Security Council from passing resolutions allowing

---

[65] 27 World Countries Attending Tehran Conference on Syria, FARS, August 09, 2012
[66] Taking the lead on Syria, The Washington Post, August 09, 2012
[67] Iran's Red Crescent to dispatch humanitarian aid to Syria, Islamic Republic News Agency, May 21, 2012

foreign military intervention. Most famously, US Secretary of State Hilary Clinton threatened that Russia and China would "pay a price" for their position on the Syrian issue, prompting the Russian Foreign Ministry to categorically reject accusations of backing Bashar al-Assad and sharing complicity in bloodshed and civilian deaths in Syria.[68] While Clinton attempts to blame Russia and China for "holding up progress" in attempts to overthrow the Assad government, it is more likely that the United States' own loss of legitimacy is the reason it has not successfully convinced the world to go along with a self-serving and very untenable agenda. The ideology behind the Russian and Chinese foreign policy is best summarized by China's ambassador to the United Nations, Li Baodong:

We [do] not have intention to protect anybody against anybody. What we really want to see is that the sovereignty of that country can be safeguarded, and the destiny of that country can be in the hands of the people in Syria.[69]

The desperate defamation and threatening rhetoric of the US State Department comes at a time when the expanding Sino-Russian alliance directly impedes Western encroachment into strategically sensitive regions that are vital to the development and security of Beijing and Moscow. In stark contrast to the Western adventurism of foreign intervention under the guise of "protecting human rights" and "American principles," the diplomatic stance of the emerging Shanghai Cooperation Organization is one that values the tenets of national sovereignty over a model where outside forces dictate the future of an independent nation and its government. Although diplomatic criticisms have often been muted, Foreign Minister Sergey Lavrov has brought Russia back into the center of international decision-making with Moscow's firm stance toward the Western embrace of Syria's armed insurgents:

This is direct endorsement of terrorism. How are we supposed to understand that? This is a sinister position; I cannot find words to express our attitude towards that. In other words this means "We are going to support such acts of terrorism until the UNSC does what we want." [70]

Since reassuming his post as Russia's President, Vladimir Putin, an ardent critic of NATO's operation in Libya, has personally engaged both members of the Assad government and the opposition Syrian National Council, in addition to Turkish Prime Minister Erdoğan, Israeli Prime Minister Netanyahu, and US President Obama, in an attempt to prevent the further deterioration of the situation. Both President Putin and Foreign Minister Lavrov have shown stringent adherence to UN Envoy Kofi Annan's six point peace plan, which calls for the immediate cessation of violence, dialogue, and a UN-backed ceasefire. Putin has warned of ceaseless civil war if the Assad government is overthrown by force, urging that dialogue and pragmatism are the only means to defuse the situation:

The incumbent Syrian authorities as well as the so- called armed opposition must find strength to organize the talks and find a mutually acceptable compromise for the country's future. We believe that the following should be the course of action: halting

---

68 Clinton: Russia and China will 'pay price' for supporting Assad, Russia Today, July 06, 2012
69 China says it's not protecting Syria's Assad, AP, June 04, 2012
70 US position on Syria directly endorses terrorism - Lavrov, Russia Today, July 25, 2012

the violence, conducting negotiations, searching for a solution, laying down a
constitutional basis for the future society, and only then introducing structural
changes, not vice versa. Doing things the other way around would only cause chaos.[71]

Russia's stance reflects a growing global consensus of independent journalists and geopolitical analysts who have meticulously and objectively documented the premeditated destabilization of Syria by Western and Gulf States. Russia's ambassador to the UN, Vitaly Churkin, who urges spectators not be "duped by Western humanitarian rhetoric on Syria," reflects on the underlying aggression and deceptive nature of the dubious "Friends of Syria" group and their stance:

They have been working with the so-called 'Friends of Syria'. In fact, this is a group
of countries who are enemies of the Syrian government, I would not call them the
enemies of the Syrian people, but certainly those who want to topple the Syrian
government, disregarding the consequences which are extremely tragic; such a policy
inevitably entails [tragedy] because the government of President Assad is not simply
one individual or a group of individuals. They represent a certain segment of the Syrian
population, a certain power structure, which has existed there for decades. To break it
would cause, and is causing, considerable trouble and bloodshed. To reform it through
dialogue, this would be a much more reasonable line of action and this is what Russia
has been advocating.[72]

Apart from the moral imperative of rejecting institutionalized support for terrorism, Russia has strategic interests in maintaining their port rights to Moscow's only Mediterranean naval port in Tartus, the last remaining Russian military base outside the former Soviet Union. The naval base at Tartus has been upgraded and declared a permanent regional base for Russia's nuclear-capable warships. Western capitals have attempted to spark controversy over Russia delivering an estimated $500 million in air defense systems, reconditioned helicopters, and fighter jets to Syria. Accusations of Moscow fueling bloodshed, and the imposition of trade embargos on one of Moscow's vessels delivering Mi-25 helicopters, have driven Russia and the United States further apart diplomatically, despite the fact that contracts for Russian defense shipments to Syria were signed between 2007 and 2008.[73] In late July, Moscow agreed to delay the delivery of refurbished helicopters, while a Russian naval flotilla entered the eastern Mediterranean, consisting of 10 Russian warships and 10 escort vessels led by the Admiral Chabanenko anti-submarine destroyer, including landing ships with marines on board.[74] In May 2011, Russia's Deputy Prime Minister Dmitry Rogozin warned that, "NATO is planning a military campaign against Syria to help overthrow the regime of President Bashar al-Assad with a long-reaching goal of preparing a beachhead for an attack on Iran." He further emphasized that the NATO military alliance aims to interfere only with those states "whose views do not coincide with those of the West." Russia's Admiral Alexander Fedosenkov has said Moscow's warships in the Mediterranean are

---

[71] Putin: Non-stop civil war if Assad ousted, Russia Today, July 23, 2012
[72] 'Don't be duped by Western humanitarian rhetoric on Syria' – Russia's UN ambassador, Russia Today, July 20, 2012
[73] Russia Will Delay Delivery of Helicopters to Syria, The Moscow Times, July 20, 2012
[74] Russian flotilla headed for Syria enters Mediterranean, Yahoo News, July 24, 2012

preparing for naval drills scheduled for September 2012, and are not carrying out any military tasks in Syria.[75]

Despite a long history of mutual distrust between Russia and China, both nations have a common interest in growing their economic sectors and resisting American military expansion in their spheres of influence. Following the announcement that the United States plans to shift 60 percent of its warships to the Asia-Pacific, Moscow announced that it would boost military cooperation with Beijing, including holding more joint exercises, giving way to Sino-Russian naval exercises in the Yellow Sea held during April 2012.[76] Foreign Minister Lavrov has emphasized the strong opposition of both Moscow and Beijing against the efforts of Washington and NATO to expand their military alliances by deploying missile defense systems in various parts of the world. Russia and China have spoken out against expansionism of the Western military bloc and the deployment of missile defense systems in Eastern Europe. Moscow feels threatened by the continued eastern expansion of NATO, potentially into former Soviet states that have long been viewed as Russia's traditional sphere of influence, such as Ukraine and Georgia. Elsewhere, Beijing is concerned with American military expansion into the Asia-Pacific, the continued arms sales to Taiwan, and the backing of the Philippines in the ongoing territorial dispute in the South China Sea. Russia and China intend to continue strengthening their partnership by defending each other's mutual sovereignty and territorial integrity, and by increasing bilateral trade to $100 billion by 2015. Foreign Minister Lavrov underlines the strong disapproval of both Moscow and Beijing with American hegemony and military encroachment:

Russia and China support the establishment of a multipolar model of international relations, the formation of a fairer and democratic political and economic system, the strengthening of the UN central coordinating role in solving pressing issues on the international agenda. [77]

Unsurprisingly, the leaders of Russia and China are staunchly opposed to the use of military force against Iran, as Washington and Tel Aviv continue their assertions to "keep all options open" with regard to halting the development of Tehran's nuclear program.[78] Since returning to office, President Putin has begun implementing plans to create a Russian-dominated Eurasian economic and military bloc, beginning with the formation of a bilateral Union State between Russia and Belarus, vowing to counter all foreign attempts to affect the internal affairs of that union, including limitation and sanctions. Upon taking office, President Putin emphasized the need for Moscow to further develop its nuclear arsenal, along with Russia's own air and space defenses, ordering that the development of modern weapons be increased by 75-85 per cent for the nuclear forces and to 70 per cent for space and air defense by 2020, stating:

We are not going to enter the arms race, but no one should have any doubts in the reliability and effectiveness of our nuclear potential, as well as the means of air and

[75] Russian Warships in Mediterranean 'not Engaged in Syria Tasks, RiaNovosti, July 26, 2012

[76] Putin says to push military ties with China, Reuters, June 06, 2012

[77] Russia, China Condemn West's Missile Shield Program, FARS, June 06, 2012

[78] China, Russia, Say No To War With Iran, Forbes, June 06, 2012

space defense. The nuclear weapons remain the most important guarantee of Russia's sovereignty and territorial integrity, and play a key role in maintaining the regional balance and stability.[79]

In reaction to Washington and NATO's firm aversion to cooperating with Moscow on the controversial missile defense shield in Eastern Europe, Russia has begun developing its offensive weapons capability by bolstering its intercontinental ballistic missile system. Vladimir Kozin, a leading researcher at the Russian Strategic Research Institute, elaborated on the threat posed by NATO's expansion to the borders of Russian territory:

The new missile project is a step in the right direction at a time when the United States is engaged in large-scale modernization of its strategic and tactical nuclear potentials, and amid the continuing deployment of the European and global missile defense systems. Such a combination carries even more threats for Russia and its allies and friends, than a separately operating missile shield. Washington, as NATO's May summit demonstrated, continues to neglect the Russian leadership's concerns about the absolutely unjustified assembly of a multi-layered missile defense structure near the Russian borders, as well as Russia's proposals to form a less provocative, but more efficient missile defense structure. [80]

President Obama has supported the construction of an anti-ballistic missile system in Eastern Europe to safeguard against a possible strike from Iran. Initially, Moscow pressed NATO officials for a guarantee that this AMB system would not be used to target Russia, something that officials were unable to legally guarantee.[81] In response, former Russian President Dmitry Medvedev warned, "Russia will deploy modern offensive weapons systems in the west and south of the country, thereby ensuring its ability to take out any part of the US missile defense system in Europe." Medvedev also hinted at Moscow's withdrawal from the Strategic Arms Reduction Treaty signed in 2010, an initiative to mutually reduce nuclear stockpiles in the United States and Russia. The conflict in Syria is one of many flashpoints for increased tension and possible military exchange between Moscow and Washington. While the administrations in Moscow and Beijing are not without their own shortcomings, their stance throughout the Syrian conflict represents the increased institutional influence of emerging nations and their impact on international affairs. As members of the Shanghai Cooperation Organization focus on increasing trade, building infrastructure, and expanding mutually beneficial, peaceful economic development, President Putin's claims that the United States suffers from an "illusion of invulnerability," offers valuable insight into the shape of things to come.[82]

(August 12, 2012)

---

[79] Putin pushes nuclear, space defense reform, Russia Today, July 26, 2012

[80] New Russia weapons to counter NATO strategic fist - expert, Russia Today, May 24, 2012

[81] NATO Cannot Provide Russia with Missile Guarantees, Says Deputy Secretary General, Estonian Public Broadcasting, May 29, 2012

[82] America suffers from 'illusion of invulnerability' - Putin, Russia Today, March 02, 2012

Conclusion

"People who have been debased for so long that they have become like animals, or worse, absolutely will not demand liberty. They might avenge themselves on the despot, but this will be only to take revenge on his person, not to get rid of despotism. This will not benefit the people, for it will be exchanging one disease for another, like substituting a headache for a stomach ache."

Abd al-Rahman al-Kawakibi

Syrian Philosopher & Proponent of Pan-Islamic Arab Unity

The infinite complexities of the troubles facing Bashar al-Assad's Syria are not to be underestimated. While Damascus has responded to this campaign of insurgency much like any government would, the lack of restraint and the individual misconduct of members of the Syrian military have regrettably contributed to the loss of life. Contrary to the popular historical account of events, the conflict that has ravaged Syria is not an indigenous internal dispute, and it is not a tale of a belligerent dictator bent on "murdering his own people." Regardless of how this situation is resolved, it must be remembered as an attempt by allied foreign entities to use unrestrained tactics of subversion and terrorism to overthrow a sovereign nation's government. While the official casualty rates offered by the United Nations remain highly questionable, those innocents who suffered untimely deaths at the expense of this state-sponsored destabilization campaign must not be forgotten. If any political transition takes place in Syria, it must be through dialogue and not through force. Before any such transition occurs, it is the responsibility of the Syrian government to restore order and safety to the civilian population. As allied foreign nations convene together to decide the fate of Damascus, it would be appear that the right of Syria's own people to decide their political destiny has been overlooked.

Syria's people must collectively decide the future of their nation, and the fate of Bashar al-Assad. As the northern city of Aleppo becomes the epicenter of insurgency in the eighteenth month of the conflict, attention must be lent to one of Syria's most prominent intellectuals, a man who would be most concerned with the violence engulfing his birthplace if he were alive today. Abd al-Rahman al-Kawakibi was born in Aleppo in 1849, and was a leading proponent of secularism and unity throughout the Arab world. The nationalistic components of al-Kawakibi's philosophy of unity, freedom, and socialism contributed to the ideological foundations of Arab leaders such as Gamal Abdel Nasser, and later to the Syrian Ba'ath party. Al-Kawakibi spoke ardently of his repugnance for autocracy, but warned, "despotism must be fought not with violence but, rather, with gradualism and gentleness." Despotism, as he perceived it, cannot be overthrow by force, at risk of "substituting a headache for a stomach ache." Al-Kawakibi instead favored evolutionary and incremental change, and the transformation of society at large through education.

Al-Kawakibi was troubled by what he saw as the decline of Islamic communities, but unlike other thinkers of his day, he attributed this trend not to external forces, but to reactionary Muslim despots. The theories of Al-Kawakibi remain strikingly relevant to the present situation, where disunity and sectarian violence plague much of the Islamic world. Muslims and worshippers of all backgrounds must take heed to avoid enflaming such social and religious differences, as these sectarian distinctions have been historically exploited by colonial and imperialist powers to turn communities against each other. Much can be drawn from Al-Kawakibi's assessments of political despotism, for if the secular Syrian state is shattered, the political entity that replaces it may prove be infinitely more self-serving and despotic. Syrian people face a difficult choice and an uncertain future, one that will have enormous ramifications both regionally and domestically. If external actors impose "democracy" on the Syrian state, the resulting political order that emerges will unquestionably operate as a vassal of those foreign entities that fed the insurgency and violence at the expense of innocent lives.

An article published by *Foreign Policy* in late July 2012 titled, "Inside the quiet effort to plan for a post-Assad Syria," lays bare the methodology being used by the United States to establish a client regime in Damascus.[1] The US State Department, through the "United States Institute of Peace" is working directly with Syrian opposition groups to formulate a new Syrian constitution, referred to as a "transition strategy document." The United States Institute of Peace is a direct functionary of the American government, with acting members of the US State Department, including Michael Posner and members of the US Department of Defense, including James Miller, serving on the USIP Board of Directors. Such admissions exhibit the absolute illegitimacy of the so-called "Syrian opposition," - a complete contrivance of the US government, and in no way representative of the Syrian people. The unparalleled criminality of Washington is nowhere more apparent than in the *New York Times'* outrageous article, "US to Focus on Forcibly Toppling Syrian Government," which is all but an admission that indeed, foreign-backed terrorists have failed, and that the restoration of order by the Syrian army is imminent:

> *The Obama administration has for now abandoned efforts for a diplomatic settlement to the conflict in Syria, and instead it is increasing aid to the rebels and redoubling efforts to rally a coalition of like-minded countries to forcibly bring down the government of President Bashar al-Assad, American officials say. "We're looking at the controlled demolition of the Assad regime," said Andrew J. Tabler, a Syria expert at the Washington Institute for Near East Policy. "But like any controlled demolition, anything can go wrong."* [2]

In Syria, things have gone very wrong, and the rhetoric being espoused to justify the malicious conduct of Washington's foot soldiers is nothing sort of alarming.

Perhaps the most damning example of editorial dishonesty comes from Ed Husain, senior fellow for Middle Eastern Studies at the US Council on Foreign Relations. His August 2012 article, "Al-Qaeda's Specter in Syria," argues in favor of al-Qaeda terrorists and their inclusion in the Free Syrian Army, in what can be categorized only as an attempt to project cognitive dissonance to his readership, a

---

[1] Inside the quiet effort to plan for a post-Assad Syria, Foreign Policy, July 20, 2012
[2] US to Focus on Forcibly Toppling Syrian Government, The New York Times, July 22, 2012

state in which an individual holds two conflicting ideas simultaneously in a consistent belief system:

The Syrian rebels would be immeasurably weaker today without al-Qaeda in their ranks. By and large, Free Syrian Army (FSA) battalions are tired, divided, chaotic, and ineffective. Feeling abandoned by the West, rebel forces are increasingly demoralized as they square off with the Assad regime's superior weaponry and professional army. Al-Qaeda fighters, however, may help improve morale. The influx of jihadis brings discipline, religious fervor, battle experience from Iraq, funding from Sunni sympathizers in the Gulf, and most importantly, deadly results. In short, the FSA needs al-Qaeda now.[3]

To argue in favor of the same terrorist entity that was used to justify over a decade of American presence in Iraq, Afghanistan, and elsewhere, is a wanton display of hypocrisy and academic irresponsibility. Clearly, no nation could, in good conscience, or in the interest of self-preservation, condone the overt destabilization of Syria by foreign powers with disingenuous motives, using listed terrorist organizations to do so. Husain's commentary is a testament to the desperate and bizarre illogicality of the US position on Syria, characterized by a willingness to sponsor the very monsters against whom Washington has long cried foul.

To follow suit, *Foreign Policy* published an August 2012 article literally titled, "Two Cheers for Syrian Islamists." Author Gary Gambill, General Editor of the Neo-Con Middle East Forum, concedes that the Syrian government "would not be in the trouble it's in today were it not for the Islamists," revealing what the allied foreign powers and their media houses have attempted but failed at obfuscating - that the violence in Syria is the work of sectarian extremists, not "pro-democracy activists." The latter's existence was amplified by the Western media specifically to provide cover and legitimacy for the violence and subversion of the former. Gambill continues his "two cheers" for terrorism in perhaps the most perverse statement found to-date in the Western press on the subject:

Islamists – many of them hardened by years of fighting U.S. forces in Iraq – are simply more effective fighters than their secular counterparts. Assad has had extraordinary difficulty countering tactics perfected by his former jihadist allies, particularly suicide bombings and roadside bombs. [4]

Gambill is effusively praising men who have killed his own nation's solders, admiring their prowess on the battlefield through their use of indiscriminate terrorist tactics, which have killed and maimed tens of thousands of civilians across the Arab World. Gambill disingenuously claims that Washington can do "little about" what he calls the "political ascendancy" of these sectarian extremists, portraying the rise of violence across the Levant and the miraculous resurrection of the Muslim Brotherhood across the Arab World as coincidentally aligned to American interests:

So long as Syrian jihadis are committed to fighting Iran and its Arab proxies, we should quietly root for them – while keeping our distance from a conflict that is going

[3] Al-Qaeda's Specter in Syria, The Council on Foreign Relations, August 06, 2012
[4] Two Cheers for Syrian Islamists, Foreign Policy, August 23, 2012

to get very ugly before the smoke clears. There will be plenty of time to tame the beast after Iran's regional hegemonic ambitions have gone down in flames.

It must be remembered that the terrorists Gambill is "cheering" for have destroyed peaceful communities, committed racially and religiously motivated violence and ensnared millions of Western troops for over a decade in the oxymoronic and fictitious "War on Terror," killing innumerable innocents. As public awareness grows of Western support for these very terrorists, it would be almost inconceivable that there would not be a profound, perhaps even violent backlash against people like Gambill and the establishment he represents.

Reuters's duplicitously titled August 2012 report, "Libyan freedom fighters join with Syrian rebels," confirms what independent geopolitical analysts and alternative news sources have reported for months, that members of the Libyan Islamic Fighting Group (LIFG) are stationed in Syria, and leading offensives against the Syrian government.[5] The Libyan Islamic Fighting Group is designated as an al-Qaeda affiliate by the United Nations pursuant to resolutions 1267 (1999) and 1989 (2011), noting several prominent LIFG terrorists occupying the highest echelons of al-Qaeda's command structure, in addition to being listed by both the US State Department and the UK Home Office as a foreign terrorist organization and a proscribed terrorist organization respectively.[6] In direct violation of both American and British anti-terrorism legislation, particularly provisions regarding providing material support for listed or proscribed terrorist organizations, the United Kingdom announced in August 2012 that it will provide armed militants, including listed terror organizations, with a £5 million tranche of what it calls "non-lethal practical assistance." This means that the United States, the United Kingdom, the North Atlantic Treaty Organization, with Turkey, Saudi Arabia, and Qatar are knowingly and willfully funding designated affiliates of al-Qaeda contrary not only to US and British anti-terror legislation, but contrary to UN resolutions as well.[7]

The US State Department's own website features a list of designated foreign terrorist organizations (FTO) upon which both al-Qaeda (#37) & the LIFG (#28) are clearly listed. Toward the bottom of the page, the State Department indicates the "Legal Ramifications of [its] Designation" as follows:

1. It is unlawful for a person in the United States or subject to the jurisdiction of the United States to knowingly provide "material support or resources" to a designated FTO. (The term "material support or resources" is defined in 18 U.S.C. § 2339A(b)(1) as " any property, tangible or intangible, or service, including currency or monetary instruments or financial securities, financial services, lodging, training, expert advice or assistance, safehouses, false documentation or identification, communications equipment, facilities, weapons, lethal substances, explosives, personnel (1 or more individuals who maybe or include oneself), and transportation, except medicine or religious materials." 18 U.S.C. § 2339A(b)(2) provides that for these purposes "the term 'training' means instruction or teaching designed to impart a specific skill, as opposed

---

[5] Libyan freedom fighters join with Syrian rebels, Reuters, August 18, 2012
[6] QE.L.11.01. LIBYAN ISLAMIC FIGHTING GROUP, United Nations, August 23, 2010
[7] Britain to give £5 million to Syria rebels, Times of India, August 10, 2012

to general knowledge." 18 U.S.C. § 2339A(b)(3) further provides that for these purposes the term 'expert advice or assistance' means advice or assistance derived from scientific, technical or other specialized knowledge."

2. Representatives and members of a designated FTO, if they are aliens, are inadmissible to and, in certain circumstances, removable from the United States (see 8 U.S.C. §§ 1182 (a)(3)(B)(i)(IV)-(V), 1227 (a)(1)(A)).

3. Any U.S. financial institution that becomes aware that it has possession of or control over funds in which a designated FTO or its agent has an interest must retain possession of or control over the funds and report the funds to the Office of Foreign Assets Control of the U.S. Department of the Treasury.[8]

The misconduct and criminality of both the United States and the United Kingdom with respect to aiding and abetting terrorist organizations in Syria and Libya constitute high crimes and treason. Under the anti-terrorism legislation in place in both nations, the following demands can be substantiated:

• The immediate resignation and trial of **United States Secretary of State Hillary Rodham Clinton** under the United States' USC § 2339A & 2339B - Providing material support or resources to designated foreign terrorist organizations.

• The immediate resignation and trial of **United States Ambassador to the United Nations Susan Rice** under the United States' USC § 2339A & 2339B - Providing material support or resources to designated foreign terrorist organizations.

• The immediate resignation and trial of **British Foreign Secretary and First Secretary of State William Hague** under the United Kingdom's Anti-terrorism, Crime and Security Act of 2001.

The generation preceding Hillary Clinton's, those of World War II, swore "never again" to the tragedy of that global conflict. They also swore "never again" to the lies and manipulations that maneuvered millions of people across the globe into deadly conflict with one another. Hillary Clinton's fabrications and attempts to foist yet another war constructed upon falsehoods betrays that promise, and thus jeopardizes the very foundation and principles upon which civilization stands. Hillary Clinton, to continue in her capacity, like the entire Bush Administration before her, compromises and forever stains the credibility and integrity of the United States. Not only has the Obama administration, with Hillary Clinton as Secretary of State and Susan Rice as Ambassador to the United Nations, inherited and perpetuated this violent conspiracy against the Syrian people, it has inherited and perpetuated the dishonor and straining of America's remaining integrity and global good will. For America's economy which cannot shoulder another military adventure, for America's honor which cannot find space to fit another scar, Hillary Clinton and Susan Rice must resign and those in Congress and throughout industry must withdraw support for those squandering the last of America's once vast potential in pursuit of militaristic hegemony.

---

[8] Foreign Terrorist Organizations, U.S. Department of State, January 27, 2012

While the State Department's "Legal Ramifications of [its] Designation" clearly prohibits providing "safehouses" to designated foreign terrorist organizations, American Neo-Conservatives have concurrently "called on" US President Barack Obama to assist in the establishment of "safe zones" inside of Syria in a July 2012 letter published by the "Foreign Policy Initiative" (FPI) and the "Foundation for the Defense of Democracies" (FDD). The letter, published in *Foreign Policy's* article "Conservatives call on Obama to establish 'safe zones' in Syria," was signed by co-conspirators in the invasion of Iraq including Elliott Abrams, Karl Rove, and Paul Bremer, along with advisors to Mitt Romney, including Eric Adelman and Robert Kagan.[9] Both institutions are corporate, foundation, and government-funded clearinghouses, extensions of larger think tanks like the American Enterprise Institute, responsible for manufacturing consensus behind aggressive agendas that have little to no support within the general public. Perhaps the most disturbing aspect of the open letter is its calls for a no-fly zone over Syria:

We urge you to take immediate steps, in close and continuing consultation with the Congress, to work with regional partners to establish air-patrolled "safe zones" covering already liberated areas within Syria, using military power not only to protect these zones from further aggression by the Assad regime's military and irregular forces, but also to neutralize the threat posed by the Syrian dictatorship's chemical and biological weapons.

Reuters's August 2012 article, "Securing Syria chemical weapons may take tens of thousands of troops," illustrates the frightening possibility of direct military intervention in Syria:

The United States and its allies are discussing a worst-case scenario that could require tens of thousands of ground troops to go into Syria to secure chemical and biological weapons sites following the fall of President Bashar al-Assad's government, according to U.S. and diplomatic officials.

Two diplomatic sources, also speaking on condition of anonymity, said as many as 50,000 or 60,000 ground forces may be needed if officials' worst fears are realized, plus additional support forces. Even a force of 60,000 troops, however, would not be large enough for peacekeeping and would only be the amount required to secure the weapons sites - despite some of the appearances of a Iraq-style occupation force, the diplomatic sources cautioned.[10]

Anonymous US officials cited by the *Wall Street Journal* reported that the Syrian government is taking chemical weapons out of storage for possible use "against anti-regime rebels or civilians, possibly in an ethnic cleansing campaign." [11] Despite claiming to possess this information, the US officials refused to disclose the location these weapons were being moved to, or the specific weapons, stating only "they are most worried about Syria's stockpiles of sarin gas." The Syrian government has withstood over a year of political, economic, and diplomatic attacks, both in the form of media disinformation and military subversion. The logical question one might ask would be why the Syrian government would use chemical weapons, providing the

---

[9] Conservatives call on Obama to establish 'safe zones' in Syria, Foreign Policy, July 24, 2012
[10] Securing Syria chemical weapons may take tens of thousands of troops, Reuters, August 17, 2012
[11] Annan 'appalled' by reported killings, UPI, July 13, 2012

West the pretext needed to maneuver around the obstructions posed by the lack of consensus in the UN Security Council. The answer is simple, the Syrian government is not pondering the use of chemical weapons – allied foreign powers and their terrorist proxies are. Washington has long talked of "tipping the balance" of the conflict to their favor, and it appears highly plausible that the threat of chemical weapons and their use may be used to justify forcibly toppling Damascus.

From the start of the conflict in Syria, the possibility of open foreign military intervention has loomed uncomfortably over the series of diplomatic measures taken in an attempt to diffuse the situation – those efforts have now deteriorated. Given the unpredictability of the Syrian situation, it is difficult to foresee any possible outcomes to the ongoing crisis, though the possibility of the following situations coming to pass, and their ramifications, must be considered:

• **Assad attempts to quell the insurgency by force**, reflecting the conduct of nations such as Algeria, who have successfully suppressed insurgents affiliated with AQIM. This course of action may work to further enflame the situation if outside forces continue to increase their use of foreign mercenaries and provide rebel fighters with more dangerous armaments, including chemical or biological weapons. If Syrian security forces are unable to restore order and crush the insurgency, any authentic or manufactured atrocity or incursion into Turkish territory may be enough to tip the scale in favor of open military intervention (with or without the approval of the UNSC). If that occurs, the Turkish-Syrian border would see open exchanges of fire, with Ankara attempting to capture territory in northern Syria. Iran would likely offer military support to Assad, while the non-interventionist policies of Russia and China make their actions more difficult to foresee. From that point, the potential for a wider regional conflict is plausible.

• **Assad succeeds in quelling the insurgency by force**, causing rebel militants to disperse, surrender and take refuge in rural areas and neighboring countries. Syrian security forces would increase their operations and attempt to maintain order in population centers. The military would secure tense areas and some form of normality would resume, although bombings, border incursions and other attacks could persist on a smaller scale. Assad would step up internal security, and be demonized as an international pariah. Syria would continue suffering under heavy economic sanctions. If Assad continues to hold onto power and fails to deliver meaningful reforms and political pluralism, internal dissent could again become problematic, potentially shifting moderates to embrace factions of the opposition. Political turmoil would ensue, but the security situation could be stabilized if insurgent activity is successfully subdued.

• **Assad's government collapses by force**, either from being overtaken by rebel forces or as a result of foreign military intervention. If insurgents pushed forward with their campaign and were able to capture territory and maintain an upper hand, armed gangs could persecute Assad loyalists, Alawites, Shi'as, and other religious minorities such as Christians and Druze, reflecting the conduct of Libyan LIFG fighters following the fall of Gaddafi. Chemical weapons may be used by the rebels to incriminate Assad and justify intervention, or legitimately used by Assad to repel foreign military forces entering the country *en masse*. The resulting interim government would struggle to maintain the security situation and likely be unable to implement coherent policy amid divisions in leadership. Political turmoil would ensue, and armed gangs could continue their campaign, amid increasing sectarian tensions. The long-term ramifications of this scenario are difficult to imagine, but it would likely be characterized by volatility and incredible human suffering if the situation becomes an extended conflict.

The global hegemony of Wall Street and London has been built behind a facade of "human rights," "freedom," and "democracy." As contemporary Western civilization is characterized by the erosion of these very principles, their use for disguising imperialism, corporate monopolization, and military aggression abroad have become overt and increasingly ineffective. While Washington blames Moscow and Beijing for "holding up progress" in the West's campaign of premeditated destabilization in Syria, it is more likely that the West's own loss of legitimacy is the true reason it has not successfully convinced representatives of large percentages of the global population to acquiesce to its self-serving, fabricated, and untenable agenda. Should the United States fail in its attempts to overthrow the government of Syria, and quite likely even if it does manage to succeed, the West's credibility and that of its institutions have deteriorated so significantly, that future gambits will be even more difficult to execute.

As the West's economy and geopolitical power crumbles and its reach becomes less subtle and more adversarial, shareholders will seek more secure investments: financial, political, and tactical. Maintaining an empire relies on an immense global infrastructure that the West still possesses, one that is meeting competition from both rival hegemonies and individual nations. Empires are also built on psychological factors, such as faith in one's institutions and fear of one's military prowess. The West has been increasingly faltering in all respects in a world where these concepts are becoming increasingly challenged by shifting social, economic, and technological paradigms. What the West should be doing is positioning itself for this changing world instead of clinging to a crumbling empire, scrambling to build a global paradigm rendered antiquated long before it has even been implemented. Boycotting the corporate-financier interests behind this attempt at establishing inclusive hegemony will accelerate and ensure its failure. Instead, creating genuine institutions on a local and national level for and by the people will ensure that we are not left in disarray once these corrupt international institutions are rendered obsolete.

As difficult as it might be for some to believe, Syria's problem is not violence, armed insurrection, or political upheaval. Neither is it economic or social. These are but symptoms, many purposefully induced from abroad, of Syria's real problem, and therefore any solution aimed at treating only these symptoms will provide merely the most superficial and temporary relief. Many geopolitical analysts know this, and yet champion the immediate treatment of these symptoms, particularly the end of violence, which would indeed neutralize the situation. Ultimately, however, this fails if the root of the problem is not also exposed and a solution is not formulated and appropriately promoted. Syria's problem is not the "Free Syrian Army" or the "Syrian National Council," nor is it the myriad of terrorist organizations operating under this umbrella. Instead, it is the corporate-financier driven foreign interests that created, fund, and arm these groups, tactically and politically perpetuating their activities.

Syria's problem is that it has attracted the attention of Wall Street and London and found itself in the middle of their geopolitical aspirations for global hegemony.

Analysts believe that undermining Western ambitions for regime change in Syria by immediately coming to a negotiated agreement with Syria's so-called "opposition" should take priority. Even by merely attempting to do this with some degree of credibility, it may afford Syria the time needed to retrench against foreign destabilization - even if a settlement ultimately fails. In the case of Syria, so much time has been invested in reaching a negotiated agreement, that many have lost sight of the fact that the West and its Gulf allies are creating this violence in the first place, and that their proxy "opposition" movement has rejected any and all reasonable terms of negotiated agreements specifically to avoid this reprieve in destabilization. By breaking momentum, the West fears it may be unable to recreate this subversion in the near future, should a meaningful ceasefire be established. Beyond this goal for temporary reprieve, lie solutions aimed deeper and broader, at the very base of the allied powers driving this conflict, and similar campaigns of violence and political destabilization worldwide. Identifying and exposing the compromised interests driving the governments of NATO and its mercenary proxies, institutions, NGOs, and media – organizations such as *Human Rights Watch*, *Amnesty International*, the International Criminal Court, and even the United Nations itself to a great extent – is the first step in truly solving the problems facing Syria and other nations.

Exposing these interests as the main perpetrators of Syria's premeditated campaign of violence and destabilization is an absolute necessity in any attempt to undermine the legitimacy of the West's fabricated dominant narrative. External forces must be held accountable for engaging in activities that have brought the Syrian crisis to this dismal stage. Considering the level of subversion and deceit demonstrated by foreign powers operating in Syria, Bashar al-Assad's ambitions to crush insurgent fighters by force may well be warranted. All efforts must be made to transition the Syrian people into a climate of normality, including the removal of economic sanctions. At this crucial stage, the Syrian government should exercise as much restraint as possible to ensure the safety of civilians. Until the Syrian government restores order and provides total security to its people, no viable political transitions can be agreed upon. The government of Bashar al-Assad must continue to make tangible reforms that legitimize dissent and promote expression while individuals within the "Free Syrian Army" must lay down their arms, lest they be dealt with by force. The implications of both foreign military intervention and regime change in Syria hold unacceptable consequences for the Syrian people and the entire region. Even if internal actors agree upon a solution, it will take years for the people of Syria to recover from this conflict. If the majority of the Syrian people desire a change in leadership, the world must respect their aspirations. However, such a decision can only be reached once the domestic security situation has transitioned to one of order. Those individuals who value stability founded on the pillars of peace, compromise and conflict aversion must stand with the Syrian people and help steer them out of these dark times.

(Aug. 24, 2012)

Frames from Progressive Press Hit on Youtube, "The Foreign Subversive Army Massacres its Human Shields in Daraya"

On Aug. 25, 2012 NATO-backed jihadists committed a major massacre in the Damascus suburb of Daraya. As with Houla, the mainstream media (MSM) rushed to blame the "Assad regime." On Aug. 27, Progressive Press blog "The Big Lie & Dirty War Against Syria" headlined, "MSM Close Ranks around Daraya False Flag Coverup," analyzing the evidence that the FSA were the perpetrators. On Aug. 28, a secret NATO teleconference decided on a strike against Syria, basing on the media hysteria. On Aug. 29, the first Western journalist to visit the scene, Robert Fisk, confirmed that the victims were killed before the Army came in to restore order.

Standard operating procedure: Self-styled activists (may be assets of US intel) post fake evidence to corporate media, who stir up world opinion. USA then takes actions against target nation, which are never retracted, even if media errors are. As I noted in *The War on Freedom*, this is how the US goes to war almost every time, through a coordinated campaign by the industrial-military-media complex.

In our video clip we give examples of what the MSM do and do not show:

The BBC presented this "activist photo" as piles of children's bodies slain by Bashar al-Assad. In fact it shows victims of US war crimes against Iraq.

Syria massacre in Houla condemned as outrage grows

27 May 2012

PHOTO FROM ACTIVIST

NEWS MIDDLE EAST

Home UK Africa Asia Europe Latin America Mid-East US

This image - which cannot be independently verified - is believed to show the bodies of children in Houla awaiting burial

The able-bodied Syrian people – 14 million out of a total population of 22 million nationwide – get out to rally behind their government, and to decry foreign intervention. The MSM suppress this news, and cover only their pet NATO-backed "protesters."

—John-Paul Leonard

Excerpts from Progressive Press blog, "The Big Lie and Dirty War Against Syria"

A favorite opposition argument is that peaceful protesters restrained themselves for a long time, until the "brutal crackdown by the Assad regime" stoked their rage and they started to fight back... The first fatalities in Daraa were seven policemen and four armed protesters. Some or all of the dead were shot by mysterious snipers on rooftops, who were shooting at BOTH police and protesters... The Syrian Army reported capturing one such foreign provocateur.

When you ask Syria opposition activists, "Why not give the new reforms a chance?" they often answer, "Too little, too late. We suffered 42 years under the Assad dictatorship." When you then ask why they are not supporting the protests against the reactionary Al Khalifa family of Bahrain, who have ruled there for over 200 years, you get no answer.

The word "shabiha" means ghosts, and that is what they are – the ghosts of killed or vanished FSA fighters. These "shabiha" are mythical beings, whose sole role is to propagate the myth of Assad murdering his own people, by shifting the blame for the FSA's own killings. That's why they vanish and turn into anti-government snipers at the approach of the Syrian army or even a journalist. Robert Fisk saw them in his mind's eye before he went to Daraya, but not when he got there. In the harsh light of day, he saw only anti-government snipers – indeed he had to dodge their fire.

The time has come to rename the MSM, or Mainstream Media, as the MMM – the Mass Murdering Media.

Destroy the country in order to bring in corrupt Allied corporations to rebuild it – or more likely run it into a hellhole like Somalia, Libya or Afghanistan. The ploy should be clear to any reader of the best-seller, *Economic Hit Man*, with its lesson that America's foreign policy is foreign plunder. It's no fount of donations, to pay public sector employees, of all things, as in the SNC fairyland fantasy, which targets the juveniles and "revtards" (retarded revolutionaries) who make up the FSA supporter base worldwide.

The evil of corruption on this planet has got to be most putrid at the apex of empire, the USA, where vulture capital rules the roost... At least Syria has its own phones, and phone bills go to pay Syrian workers. If Syria is defeated, it will become just another kleptocratic colony, run by "democratic" puppets who sell out their country.

Endangering civilians by mounting a guerrilla warfare operation in cities and towns is a war crime in itself.

www.ingramcontent.com/pod-product-compliance
Lightning Source LLC
LaVergne TN
LVHW080739290126

830673LV00022B/2373